ENDORSEMENTS

Holy Covenant is a powerful devotional born out of deep pain, unshakable faith, and supernatural encounter. In these pages, Amanda Hill invites believers into a place where communion becomes more than a ritual—it becomes a lifeline, a war strategy, and a doorway into the Presence of God. Through the heartbreak of losing a stillborn daughter and the later loss of her husband, she discovered the healing, restoring, miracle-working power of the body and blood of Jesus. This 30-day journey will equip you to draw near to God, personalize His covenant names, and rise in victory through guided prayer, worship, and prophetic communion. I wholeheartedly recommend this book to every believer hungry for deeper intimacy, healing, and triumph.

Bishop Jane Hamon

Senior Co-Leader, Vision Church, Santa Rosa Beach, FL

Amanda Hill's book, ***Holy Covenant***, will change your life! Whether you read it each day as a devotional or use it to study, she has hit a vein of the Spirit that will bring healing and transformation in your life.

Prophet Cindy Jacobs

Co-Founder Generals International, Dallas, TX

In ***Holy Covenant***, Amanda Hill has given the Body of Christ a beautiful gift. This 30-day devotional is more than a journey of reading; it is a journey of remembrance, restoration, and renewal. As you walk through these pages, you are drawn into the sacred act of communion, not as a ritual, but as a life-giving encounter with the Presence of the Lord. Amanda reminds us that our weapon of warfare is not carnal, but mighty through God. Communion is not only the table of remembrance, but also the table of victory. In the fellowship of His Body and Blood, we discover that our Mighty Warrior draws near, fights on our behalf, and heals the hidden places of our soul. This devotional will lead you into deeper intimacy with Christ and reveal the power that flows when His covenant is written on your heart. If you are longing for healing, wholeness, and the strength to overcome, ***Holy Covenant*** is a timely companion for your spiritual journey.

Pastors Aaron and Amanda Crabb
Senior Leaders, Restoring Hope Church

This is not just another book. It is the living testimony of a woman who has walked the very truths she writes about. Within these pages, covenant, communion, and the unshakable faithfulness and power of God come alive—central to the heartbeat of our faith. What makes this book extraordinary is not only the message, but the messenger: a woman of passion and truth, a prophetic voice who carries deep revelation because she has lived it. This is more than words on a page; it is the story of one who truly knows God, and it will stir your spirit to the core.

Apostle Barbara Yoder
Senior Leader, Shekinah Christian Church, Ann Arbor, MI

This book is a journey into the heart of the Lord. Amanda Hill brings deep insight that will draw you into a profound understanding of your **Holy Covenant** with the Lord. As you receive daily communion with Him, the insights you will receive will release greater covenant blessings over your life. This is your invitation to a divine exchange that will transform your life.

Apostles Pasqual and Norma Urrabazo
Co-Founders, Beautiful Life Global

I remember the moment that God connected my heart to Amanda Hill, and it changed the course of my life forever. In April of 2020, I received a message: "Hi Tricia, it's Amanda Hill. I've received a word from the Lord for you, would it be ok if I sent it?"

My response was a resounding "Yes, please!!" The word was powerful! A new anointing, a fresh mandate, and a call to push into realms that I had never been before! However, that's when everything changed. More often than not, on the heels of a transformational word of the Lord, comes a real season of resistance and an opportunity to persevere against great adversity.

In July of 2020, my world shattered with one phone call. "Tests confirm that it is cancer." My husband of twenty-eight years had just received the worst news of his life, and I felt the breath leave my body. I reached out to Amanda to pray. Immediately, she went to intercession but more than that, she gifted me a weapon: pages of a chapter in her unreleased book *Holy Pillow Talk*. The words were unpolished, unedited, and raw, "Allow the body and the blood of Jesus to go ahead of you and do war on your behalf." It was the blueprint and strategy for wielding the weapon of communion, setting my spirit on fire. The elements were sometimes very unconventional—a cookie and Kool-Aid or bread and iced tea in an Outback restaurant. I would take the elements, step into the body and blood of Jesus, and let its wonderworking power defeat every onslaught of the enemy on my husband's body. In short, victory was sealed over our family. The spirit of infirmity that had come to kill, steal, and destroy was defeated. Had it not been for communion, we may have battled longer and needlessly to win the war.

When Amanda told me that the Lord had mandated her to write a follow-up to *Holy Pillow Talk*, expounding upon the Lord's Supper and its covenant with mankind, I was ecstatic! Experiencing what this understanding had done in my life, I knew that it was going to be revolutionary in the hands of God's army. Instead of the obligatory religious ceremony that we did on Easter and Christmas, communion would become an entrance into the understanding of the undefeated weapon of warfare that would strike down every single attack from the dark kingdom against the children of God.

Holy Covenant: Triumphantly Warring with the Body and Blood of Jesus, 30 Days of Communion is a Holy Spirit-breathed look into the act of stepping into, receiving, and agreeing with the Lord's Supper in a way that it's never been taught before. The breakdown of applying the Old Testament Jewish customs, the Hebrew names of God, and the modern-day understanding of communion is going to be an instruction manual for the Body of Christ for generations to come.

Apostles Todd and Tricia Turnbow

Senior Co-Leaders, The Worship Center, Lubbock, TX

Amanda Hill unveils the depths of God's covenant with us, offering daily morsels of revelation that awaken resurrection life in the everyday. Whether you're walking through relational heartbreak, uncertainty about the future, or life-altering medical reports, wholeness remains your inheritance. ***Holy Covenant*** equips you to wage war from a place of confidence—teaching you to win your battles by appropriating the power of communion and the unbreakable covenant God has made with you.

Apostle Michele Jackson
Senior Leader, Hope Christian Church, Beltsville, MD

HOLY COVENANT

TRIUMPHANTLY WARRING WITH THE BODY AND BLOOD OF JESUS

HOLY COVENANT

TRIUMPHANTLY WARRING WITH THE BODY AND BLOOD OF JESUS

30 DAYS OF COMMUNION

AMANDA HILL

FOREWORD BY CHUCK D. PIERCE

HOLY COVENANT

TRIUMPHANTLY WARRING WITH THE BODY AND BLOOD OF JESUS

AMANDA HILL

Published by:
Hill House Enterprises, LLC

Book Design by Yvonne Parks at PearCreative.ca
Edited by Kristen Campbell and Darya Crocket

Contact Amanda Hill at www.AmandaHill.org

ISBN: 978-1-7368190-4-3 (paperback)
ISBN: 978-1-7368190-5-0 (ebook)

This book is dedicated to the man of my dreams—the one I have loved and prophesied I would marry since I was eleven years old, Reverend Dr. David Hill.

You are the love of my life, my greatest champion, now backing me from the Throne Room of Heaven. Thank you for passionately loving, endlessly supporting, zealously encouraging, and assertively pushing me, even when I resisted.

This journey has not unfolded as I envisioned. I am so grateful that this world is not eternity. I miss you every day; twenty-six years together was not enough time.

Sometimes I can almost hear your rich, chest-toned lead vocals roaring loudest as the great cloud of witnesses cheers us on.

I know you're probably saying, "It's about time you wrote this book." I've had a few things going on since you graduated! Here it is. I sure hope you are proud.

This is for you, my Love.

I love you MOST!

CONTENTS

ACKNOWLEDGMENTS AND SPECIAL THANKS

Eliana, thank you for motivating me the way your daddy would have. I appreciate all the endless encouragement, farm maintenance assistance, fabulous suppers, somewhat painful shoulder massages, and the consistent pushing that urges me to follow the truth, ways, and life of Christ. Over the last year, when I was not traveling, I was home with my head buried in my computer, writing. Thank you for your amazing patience. I could not have done this without you. Watching you grow in your faith, becoming a devout disciple and lover of Jesus, is my greatest joy! I know your daddy is watching and overflows with joy at the incredible woman you have become. I love you, Presha.

Stephanie, you have been a true sister, a devoted friend, and a constant source of support for me. You have been a loving aunt to my children. Your administrative gifts have blessed AHM and now it's officially been "Stephanie-ified." I don't know how I would have managed the last two and a half years without you. You have been a gift to us. "Thank you" will never be enough for all you have done. Can you believe we've been friends for twenty years now? PS . . . "at times."

Susie, Anne, Jenn, MJ, Tass, Norma, Mandy, Kristi-Joy, Shell, Zell, Jackie, and the other midwives and intercessors who helped me push, THANK YOU. Your support is invaluable, and I am deeply grateful.

Thanks to Marty and Bill for your selfless intercession, prophetic encouragement, and countless phone conversations. I need and appreciate you both.

Thank you to the medical professionals who assist in keeping me healthy and able to travel: Dr. David Smith, MD; Dr. Tron Malachowski, DC; and Deja Farris, LMT. I deeply appreciate you all.

Thank you, Reverend Scott Eadie, for maintaining the farm while I travel and write.

Thank you to the donors who monthly support the call on my life through your generous giving. I pray every seed that is sown will be supernaturally multiplied back to you, pressed down, shaken together, and running over in abundance! Thank you! (You know who you are!)

Thank you to the World Changers Mentorship Group for your support, love, and prayer. Your encouragement means the world to me, and I am sincerely grateful.

Thank you to Kristen, the confident conqueror, my editor who consistently and kindly pushed me along in this process.

Thank you to Martin and Norma Sarvis for your patience with all my questions and emails. I honor your Hebraic understanding as voices in Jerusalem, the city of the Great King.

Thank you to the faithful ones who have stood by my side during my darkest hour, particularly following David's graduation. When others fled and forgot, you did not. I will always remember your kindness and compassion.

Thank you to all the churches, conference hosts, and ministry leaders who have invited me to minister at your services. I consider it an honor, and I am grateful for the opportunities. I cherish the moments of fellowship with my Kingdom Family.

Thank you to my home away from home, Glory of Zion. Special thanks to Brian, Administrator Extraordinaire. I will never know how you juggle it all. Also, thanks to Judah, all the staff and volunteers, you are my people, my tribe, and I love coming "home."

Thank you to all the endorsers: Cindy Jacobs, Barbara Yoder, Todd and Tricia Turnbow, Pasqual and Norma Urrabazo, Jane Hamon, Michele Jackson, and Aaron and Amanda Crabb for your support, time, and kindness toward me and this message of covenant.

Thank you to my apostle, Chuck Pierce, for authoring the foreword. You didn't walk away after David graduated, nor did you coddle me. You remained steadfast in your support, counsel, correction, and encouragement. Your leadership and spiritual fathering have been key to my advancement.

Finally, I want to express my gratitude to the trailblazing forerunners who have paved the way for me and the next generation of leaders. I am honored to call you friends as I glean from your wise counsel and significant history with the Lord. You are true generals. I consider it an honor to share meals with you, sit beside you at round tables, build relationships through frequent communication, and stand arm in arm together as we advance His Kingdom, running side by side. You are my heroes.

FOREWORD

Amanda Hill's book is all about covenant! If you follow her incredible *Holy Covenant* guideline for thirty days, then you will walk in triumphant faith. All warfare in the earthly realm, whether spiritual or natural, is an outgrowth of God's covenant plan of fullness for the earth and man's role in accomplishing this purpose. All discipline we go through as children of God is a result of His love for us so that we experience all the promises of His covenant. God longs to have a covenant with you personally, corporately, territorially, and generationally. Victory over all of your enemies is assured once you are in covenant with the Lord.

What is covenant? Covenant is an endless partnership or solemn and binding agreement between two or more parties. Covenant with God establishes commitment to a relationship that allows His purpose for us to be fulfilled. Covenant with God is always initiated by God Himself. We cannot manipulate God in this respect. We cannot go to Him and say, "Here's our proposal; You agree with what we want to accomplish." God sets the boundaries of His agreement in the earth realm, and we are responsible to operate within those boundaries.

In this book, Amanda uses the Names of God—who He is on our behalf—in a powerful way to bring us into a deeper dialogue and communion with I AM. God created man to come into agreement with Him and to communicate His will so that man could become "the keepers of His earth." When Adam and Eve broke the conditions of the initial covenant, their disobedience necessitated an expression of God's redemptive purpose for the human race in the form of redemptive covenants and ultimately, the Messiah.

But expect warfare in order to form covenant! The enemies of God's covenant create war against those who strive to represent it in the earth. If we understand God's covenant, then we will understand the warfare around us—and it has always been intense. In the beginning, God's covenant with man was a product of boundaries, communication, and allegiance. His ultimate will was that the Garden of Eden, where man communed with Him and experienced His glory, would spread across the earth. In the end, the war will be the same. Will mankind commune with God through His Son, the Lord Jesus Christ, to release glory in the earth realm?

One of my favorite sayings is, "But God!" He is determined to align us with all that is in His heart. Therefore, God's pursuit of man includes a covenant that will produce the fullness of His plan in the earth. This everlasting covenant, the final alignment between God and man, is the most comprehensive expression of God's creative and redemptive purposes for humanity. This expression culminated in a Messiah who could redeem all the losses incurred by mankind's weakness. Though in the first covenant man failed to keep the Garden, God promises that through the final covenant of the Messiah, we have ultimate victory over our enemy, the devil! (Gen. 3:15).

Holy Covenant: Triumphantly Warring with the Body and Blood of Jesus is a communion journey like no other. I highly recommend Amanda Hill and this book as a covenant companion for you as you read your Bible and war with His Body and Blood.

DR. CHUCK D. PIERCE
President of Glory of Zion International,
Kingdom Harvest Alliance

PREFACE

Since 2002, I have experienced multiple encounters, visions, dreams, and revelations centered around **Our Holy Covenant** with Jesus, the Passover Lamb. Many incredible books have been written over the years about how remembering His sacrifice can heal our bodies. However, there are many more blessings beyond physical healing that are available for us to access. These blessings are directly connected to meditating on His atonement and receiving His pierced Body and shed Blood through communion.

Holy—(adjective) sacred, divine, or consecrated; dedicated or devoted to the service of God; having a spiritually pure quality. Covenant—(in Hebrew *Karath Berith*) to cut until the blood flows.

Jesus established and fulfilled His ***Karath Berith,*** or "**Holy Covenant**," with us through His sacrifice on the cross of Calvary, where He pledged His own Body and Blood to redeem us from the curse of sin and death.

Passover/The Feast of Unleavened Bread, the breaking of bread, and communion are all rooted in covenant and point to Jesus's ultimate sacrifice. Where Passover was celebrated, bread was broken, wine was served, communion was observed, and blessings manifested after each divine encounter. These same blessings that enveloped the faithful throughout the Old and New Testaments are also yours to receive today when you remember His sacrifice by observing communion!

Yehovah applied the steps of ancient covenant-making to the New Covenant He made with us using the bruised Body and shed Blood of Yeshua, His Son, the Passover Lamb. This process was accomplished through Jesus's Messianic acts during his final days on Earth, which established the New Covenant. King Jesus fully satisfied the requirements that make a covenant legal and binding. The next section (the seven points)[1] provides vital insights, highlighting how ancient and biblical covenants were established and how Jesus fulfilled these necessary terms with His sacrifice.

1. Covenant Terms

Before a covenant was ratified, the terms, which included promises, blessings, and curses related to the covenantal contract, were thoroughly discussed, weighed, and agreed upon by the two parties.

In the New Covenant, Jesus represents both parties, God and man (Philippians 2:5–8). He reigns as our King, serves as our High Priest, and acts as our Mediator with the Father (Hebrews 8:1–6). In Matthew 16:24–27 and Luke 14:25–35, Jesus clearly outlines the cost of being a true disciple, which may involve suffering, persecution, and injustice. However, the countless blessings far outweigh the costs for those who have said "yes" to receiving Jesus as their Savior and Lord. Eternal life,

---

1 Rick Renner and Denise Renner. "Components of a Covenant." *YouTube*, uploaded by Renner Ministries, 16 Mar. 2020, www.youtube.com/watch?v=1CExEd4M_SY.

heavenly rewards, friendship with God, and indescribable joy are just a few of His promises to us!

2. Covenant Sacrifice

Ancient cultures believed there was life in the blood. Establishing a covenant required the shedding of blood; therefore, an animal was sacrificed. The animal was cut along its backbone, and the two halves were laid open opposite each other.

In the New Covenant, Jesus is the sacrifice, the Lamb of God Who takes away the sins of the world (John 1:29). He is the Suffering Servant described in Isaiah 53, who was wounded, crushed, and pierced for us.

3. Covenant Gift Exchange

Covenant parties exchanged meaningful items such as robes, swords, bows, or belts, symbolizing their commitment to live together as one rather than independently. Robes signify identity and authority, weapons signify power and protection, and belts or girdles represent possessions and wealth.

In the New Covenant, Jesus showers us with His beautiful gifts! He takes our sin and shame and gives us His robe of righteousness, restoring our identity and authority in the Father. He destroys our weaknesses by granting us His strength, power, and protection. He dismantles poverty by becoming poor so that we can live abundantly blessed.

4. Covenant Blood Walk

To emphasize the seriousness of the covenant, both parties would participate in walking around and through the pieces of the sacrificed animal, creating a figure-eight path, which flowed with the animal's blood. As they walked around and through the death remains, pronouncing aloud the terms of the treaty, the covenant was consummated.

The figure-eight walking pattern symbolizes eternity and the continuous cycle of life, death, and rebirth. This path represented their oath to uphold their obligations to the covenant and each other, even to the extent of sacrificing their own life, if necessary.

In the New Covenant, Jesus walked the *Via Dolorosa*, which means "painful path" in Latin. This trail, marked by His own Blood, was the route He trod to the Cross of Calvary. As He carried the crossbeam, which weighed between seventy and ninety pounds, He staggered from the scourging at the hands of the Roman whip embedded with metal, nails, and bone shards. The extreme loss of Blood ensured that at each place His feet touched, His Blood spilled along the path.

5. Covenant Seal

In an ancient covenant, once the first four steps were completed, the two parties would seal their solemn pact with a special ritual, serving as a sacred reminder. Often, this ritual involved cutting themselves and then dropping a few drops of their blood into a cup of wine. Then, they would partake in the mixture of wine and the other party's blood, representing their bond. However, Jewish Law prohibited consuming blood; therefore, biblical covenants were sealed with wine, symbolizing blood.

This mutual exchange was referred to in ancient cultures as "a covenant of brotherhood," becoming flesh and blood with one another. When an individual offered their blood in a covenant, they essentially pledged their life to the other.

For the covenants that commingled blood and wine, sharp blades made incisions, which healed into lasting scars. These scars became visible and tangible testimonies marked in their skin, reminding them of the bond of covenant that had been forged.

In the New Covenant, the priceless Blood of Jesus served as the ultimate seal of our redemption. In John 6, He stated that we cannot be partakers with Him unless we drink His Blood, referring to the ancient ritual of commingled wine and blood. Even today, Jesus bears the indelible marks of His covenant with us in His Body: His nail-scarred feet and wrists, the deep wound in His side from the piercing spear, and the scars all over His Body from the torture inflicted by the Roman soldiers. Through His sacrifice, we have been brought into a "covenant of brotherhood" that results in a spiritual transformation, akin to a blood transfusion, stemming from our legal agreement with Him.

6. Covenant Name Change

In ancient cultures, when someone took someone else's blood, even wine representing blood, they acquired that individual's life, personality, character, nature, and authority. This act implied a merging of identities, essentially the two becoming one.

In the New Covenant, Jesus speaks with His disciples in John 14:13–14, stating, "And I will do whatever you ask in My Name as My representative, this I will do, so that the Father may be glorified and celebrated in the Son. If you ask Me anything in My Name, I will do it." In this passage, He reminds them and us of the benefits of entering into a covenant with Him. He takes our lives, and in return, we gain His, which includes the power and privilege to use His Name. Essentially, Jesus is saying, "As you partake of My Blood and say 'yes' to this covenant with Me, I am authorizing you to use My Name because we are one."

7. Covenant Meal

Ancient covenants were celebrated by enjoying a meal together. Bread and wine were shared, representing the body and the blood of the parties involved in the cutting of the covenant. During this triumphant occasion, the covenant partners declared their vow to live as one for the final time. Traditionally, the bread was served first at a meal where a newly formed covenant was established, followed by the wine. The bread symbolized the person's flesh and wealth and possessions, conveying the message, "All I have belongs to you." This promise was central to the covenant ritual. The wine represented the person's sacrifice, declaring, "I will give my blood to empower and fulfill the promise I made to you."

In the New Covenant, Jesus used the elements of bread and wine when He instituted communion, also known as The Lord's Supper, before His capture and crucifixion. His words, displayed in Luke 22:14–23 and Matthew 26:20–36, reveal His determination to fulfill the will of the Father. The Lord's Supper is the New Covenant meal for all who believe in and follow Jesus, The Christ.

Communion and Revival

Finally, I want to share how revivals have often been closely linked to the celebration of communion. In the early church, communion was a significant part of weekly worship. The newly appointed apostles gathered in the temple, broke bread in private homes, and shared meals. "Breaking bread" meant that they consistently and purposefully remembered their Lord's covenant with them: "This is My body which is given for you; do this in remembrance of Me" (Luke 22:19). Jesus emphatically urged them to remember, remember, remember! He wanted them to find a way to observe this practice no matter what. It was not a one-time ritual, a foolish tradition, or a mere religious formality. For them, it was a way of life.

Holy Spirit emphasized the importance of remembering the sacrifice of the Lamb of God. This significance is highlighted in 1 Corinthians 11:23–26, where the Lord Jesus conveyed this revelation to Apostle Paul. Paul wrote, "I have handed down to you what came to me by direct revelation from the Lord Himself. The same night in which he was handed over, he took bread and gave thanks. Then he distributed it to the disciples and said, 'Take it and eat your fill. It is my body, which is given for you. Do this to remember Me.' He did the same with the cup of wine after supper and said, 'This cup seals the New Covenant with My blood. Drink it—and whenever you drink this, do it to remember Me.'"

Whenever you eat this bread and drink this cup, you retell the story, proclaiming our Lord's death until He comes. According to Paul's revelation, remembering His sacrifice by observing communion proclaims the power of His wounded Body and shed Blood until He comes again!

Early Christians stressed communion as the key to sharing in Christ's Flesh and Blood. This sacrament often included a "love feast" or a shared meal of bread and wine among baptized believers.

In 1727, in Herrnhut, Germany, the Moravians began having intense disagreements within the community of believers regarding their theological differences. These doctrinal disputes led to serious divisions and the formation of competing groups, despite their shared faith. The troubled leader, Count Nikolaus Ludwig von Zinzendorf, a German nobleman, began to emphasize the importance of Christian unity. On May 12th, the community signed the "Brotherly Agreement," committing themselves to love one another and focus on their commonalities rather than their differences.

On August 13, 1727, the Moravians gathered for a Holy Communion service. During this service, they experienced a powerful encounter with Holy Spirit, who descended upon the hundreds in attendance with fire and glory. They experienced deep conviction of sin, spiritual awakening, and supernatural unity. Due to the reconciliation and transformation within the community, this day is referred to as the "Moravian Pentecost." Following this Holy Communion service, the Moravians birthed a global missions movement and established 24/7 prayer, which continued unbroken for over one hundred years.[2]

Before the Wesleyan Revivals, John and Charles Wesley encountered a group of Moravian missionaries while sailing to Georgia in 1736. After landing, they spent additional time together. John Wesley, a key figure in the Methodist movement, had a life-changing conversion in 1738 while in London. A few months later, he visited the Moravians in Herrnhut, Germany, where he wrote, "I would gladly have spent my life here; but my Master is calling me to labor in another part of His vineyard."

Wesley's conversion experience ignited the Wesleyan revival, which played a crucial role in the Great Awakening in England and America. During the Wesleyan revivals, Wesley highlighted the significance of

---

2 Paul Peucker. "We Learned to Love." *Christian History Magazine*, no. 151, 2024, www.christianhistoryinstitute.org.

frequent communion during every worship service. He referred to it as a "grand channel" for Christians to encounter Christ.[3]

One of the earliest and largest revivals of the Second Great Awakening occurred at Cane Ridge, Kentucky, in 1801, profoundly impacting America's religious landscape. This revival began as a communion retreat, placing renewed emphasis on the Body and Blood of Jesus, which was central to the revival meetings.[4]

We have heard the promises in Scripture, such as Joel 2:28–29, "It shall come about after this that I shall pour out My Spirit on all mankind; your sons and your daughters will prophesy, your old men will dream dreams, your young men will see visions. Even on male and female servants, I will pour out My Spirit in those days." We have also heard prophetic words about a third great awakening.

What if we are on the brink of witnessing and experiencing the manifestation of these promises? What if the greatest harvest of souls is upon us? The Word of God is being preached throughout the earth, and worship is being released at an entirely new level. What are we missing? I believe we are missing the beauty of remembering His covenant with us, worthily receiving His sacrifice, and triumphantly warring with His Body and Blood to see personal and corporate revival, as well as the third great awakening across the nations of the earth!

In these last days, as we eagerly anticipate the return of our beloved Bridegroom, Jesus, remembering His sacrifice by observing communion

---

3 Steve Manskar. "A Wesleyan Practice of Holy Communion." *Discipleship Ministries*, 15 Oct. 2013, www.umcdiscipleship.org.

4 Newell D. Williams. "Cane Ridge Revival." Disciples Historical Society, www.discipleshistory.org. Originally published in *The Encyclopedia of the Stone-Campbell Movement*, edited by Douglas A. Foster et al., Eerdmans, 2004, pp. 164–66.

and receiving His beaten Body and shed Blood becomes our most potent and superior instrument of war. Honoring **Our Holy Covenant** with Him strengthens our resolve, fortifies our faith, deepens our intimacy, and unites us with the global Body of Christ as we stand arm in arm, back-to-back, taking territory and advancing His Kingdom. Nothing and no one can stop this secret weapon of remembrance. ***Holy Covenant*** is a supernaturally invincible weapon in the hands of the triumphantly warring Bride of Christ.

INTRODUCTION

Christmas Day, December 25, 2002, was our daughter Raegan Elizabeth Hill's due date. She was mine and David's second child and the first girl. I went in for a routine check-up on the 18th. During the ultrasound, they could not find her heartbeat. I vividly recall the doctor, who was a family friend, yelling for the nurse in a panic while my sister, who was home from college and accompanying me to the appointment, slid down the wall, nearly fainting from the shock.

For the next two days, I experienced a mix of faith and torment. I laid my Bible on my belly, believing nothing was impossible. Hours later, I felt Raegan moving. We arrived at the hospital on December 20. I just knew she was alive, and we were on the brink of meeting our precious miracle baby. However, I soon discovered that those sensations I had felt were not her moving; they were contractions, my body desperately trying to purge her from my womb.

Around 6:00 p.m., the world around me faded as I cradled my beautiful, stillborn baby girl in my arms for the first and the last time. David and I held her tightly and prayed over her while decreeing and believing for a miracle. I sang "You Are My Sunshine" while running my fingers through her thick, almost black hair just before the nurses came to take her to the hospital morgue. We buried Raegan on December 23, two days before Christmas.

This chapter of my life unfolded as the second most challenging and darkest season imaginable. Not only were we coping with the painful weight of burying our daughter, but during this time, we were leading worship at a local church. Just three short weeks after we laid Raegan to rest, the senior leaders demanded that we return to our regular duties as if we had not just been through heartbreaking trauma. We received a letter where they invoked the words of King David, suggesting that we follow his example in the face of his baby's death: "Arise, wipe your face, and come and worship."

I felt like my faith in Jesus was deeply shaken as I was drowning in hopelessness. I needed more time. David responded that we needed to take a few months off leading worship but would still attend services. They met our request with hostility. Instead of understanding, slander and gossip became their cruel weapons against us. "If I were in the room and could lay hands on Amanda's belly, her baby would be alive today." "If she had more faith and believed God, her baby wouldn't have died." These were just a few excruciating daggers that further gaped open our hearts' already raw, bleeding wounds.

Many nights, I was jolted awake from relentless, haunting dreams. I would get out of bed, my heart racing as I frantically searched the house for my baby. Grief was overtaking me, and my doctor, concerned about my mental well-being, suggested medication. Instead, I decided to turn to the Lord, seeking His guidance in my pain. "Holy Spirit, should I take this medication?"

"No. Do not take it."

"Okay, well, then, I need a strategy to heal because this anguish is about to take me out. I feel like I'm about to lose my mind."

In my desperation, He spoke. Holy Spirit provided me with a strategy, though it was one that I did not understand. He instructed me to remember His atoning sacrifice by observing communion. Growing up in a Pentecostal denomination, I was familiar with celebrating The Lord's Supper and participating in foot washing, but we only celebrated these events once a quarter. I had never heard of anyone taking communion at home without a church leader to guide them.

Despite my uncertainty, I decided to obey His Voice. Every morning before work, I entered Raegan's decorated nursery, worshipped, prayed, and remembered Jesus's sacrifice by receiving communion. What started as simple obedience, repeated for months, surprisingly became my lifeline. Remembering and meditating on Him became my focus, my everything, my life. At first, I tried to keep it hidden from everyone, including David. I knew what I was doing was unorthodox, and I feared some might consider it heretical. However, my time with Him began to show in my words and behavior. People began to notice the shift in me. It was working. He was working. The transformative power of His covenant, remembering His Body and Blood, was changing me, healing me.

This pain birthed this book.

In early spring 2003, I was still honoring Jesus's covenantal sacrifice every morning in Raegan's nursery when I learned from my maternal grandfather during a family gathering about my family's deep Jewish roots and ancestry. For several months prior, I had been studying Jewish culture and traditions, and my grandfather's revelation motivated me to delve even deeper. A few weeks later, I attended my first Messianic Passover Seder. David was unsure about this new revelation, so I ended up attending alone. I was hungry to learn. Therefore, it did not bother me.

The rabbi began his teaching about matzah, the unleavened bread of affliction, as described in Deuteronomy 16:3. He held it up for everyone to see and began to explain the connection between the matzah and Jesus, the Christ, based on Isaiah 53.

Jesus was without sin. Throughout Scripture, leaven symbolizes sin. Since matzah contains no leaven, it represents purity.

Jesus's Body was striped from the scourging. Roman soldiers beat him with a whip that contained metal, nails, and bone shards. Consequently, due to the baking process, matzah appears striped.

Jesus was pierced. The soldiers nailed his wrists and feet to the cross, and they pierced his side with a spear, and Blood and water flowed. Matzah has small, perforated holes, which reflect this aspect of Jesus's suffering.

When the rabbi concluded this portion of the Seder, I gained a whole new understanding, as if I was Cleopas or the other disciple (Luke 24) who had walked with Jesus on the road to Emmaus. Like them, with the breaking of the bread, my eyes were now open to see Him. And it felt like it was for the very first time. I was so overcome with emotion that I struggled to hold myself together, and people began to turn around and stare. I was utterly undone. I had been receiving His wounded Body for months in Raegan's nursery. Still, it was only now that I genuinely began to grasp the profound significance of why remembering His sacrifice was so powerful. With eyes swollen and bloodshot from tears, I wept on and off for days following the Seder.

This undoing birthed this book.

In November 2017, the Lord directed me to begin remembering His atonement by receiving communion daily. He was adamant that the warfare in my life was about to intensify and that His Body and Blood would serve as my weapons. I started well, but I waned considerably as the holidays passed from one to another. In February 2018, I had a significant dream that I remember vividly.

In my dream, I found myself in my kitchen when a dark power began to attack me. Like any good Southern cook, I grabbed my frying pan and began to beat this demonic force in the head. I managed to wound it, but I could never kill it. As I struggled, I realized I was wearing myself out.

The next morning, I woke up feeling beat up—physically, emotionally, and spiritually. My arm, which I had used in the dream, ached. I chuckled to myself while remembering the encounter. I immediately heard the Lord say, "This is what you have been doing recently. You have been fighting against this new enemy with old weapons. Months ago, I instructed you to remember My covenant and what I paid for. My Body and Blood wars, speaks, sings, declares, and decrees for you. Your former weapons are not working. Use Mine."

Of course, He was absolutely right. I had been engaged in an intense battle of spiritual warfare that was taking a toll on me. This dream was a powerful illustration of my spiritual battle. I was relying on and using old, ineffective weapons in this new war that wore me down and left me exhausted. As a result, I was losing territory.

This warfare birthed this book.

After this profound dream, I was compelled to study communion, but first, I had to research the biblical and ancient roots of covenant. Covenant is foundational to understanding Passover, communion, and the breaking of bread, as they are all rooted in covenant. Without the foundational feast of Passover (*Pesach* in Hebrew), Jesus would never have had an opportunity to institute The Lord's Supper, commonly known as communion. Essentially, communion serves as a condensed or abbreviated version of Passover.

As I immersed myself in the Scriptures, I purposely and meticulously sought out every reference related to Passover, communion, and the breaking of bread, discovering the subsequent blessings and life-changing benefits that followed those who engaged in these holy encounters throughout the Old and New Testaments. This journey has powerfully transformed me. I have found that each biblical mention of Passover, communion, or the breaking of bread carries revolutionary significance for us personally, as well as for the corporate Body of Christ, the *Ekklesia*.

This revelation birthed this book.

David, my husband of twenty-five years, graduated to his eternal reward on Father's Day, June 18, 2023. The two and a half years that followed were a relentless torrent of trials. In the aftermath of his passing, I faced overwhelming abandonment. Friends, family, ministry leaders, and peers—many I had relied upon—seemed to vanish just when I needed them the most. Their absence felt like a crushing betrayal during the most horrific and vulnerable time of my life.

Just when I thought the storm was starting to weaken, I was hit with a frivolous lawsuit, a wave of character assassination, mounting family drama, and financial uncertainty. I was responsible for caring for my elderly mother-in-law, who sadly passed a year later. All of this unfolded while I was juggling the demands of maintaining a ninety-five-acre farm, running my own business, and ministering across the United States two to three weekends out of the month.

The weight of these unyielding trials began to take a severe toll on my mental and physical well-being. I found myself battling heart palpitations, struggling to breathe deeply, experiencing sleepless nights, and suffering from crippling anxiety, all while mourning my husband.

There were several occasions when I felt as though I was genuinely losing my mental stability. One night after a service, while I was alone in another state, restless in my hotel room, Holy Spirit reminded me of the revelation of remembering Jesus's covenant bought by His sacrifice through observing communion. I grabbed the gift basket the church left in the room and began digging through it to find something—anything—that would allow me to meditate on and receive His pierced Body and shed Blood. I discovered a small bag of Doritos and some coconut water, and yes, that is precisely what I used. The elements are symbolic. Jesus wants us to remember what He did. He is certainly not religious about what specific crackers or juice we use.

I took a few moments to use my imagination, a gift that He created within all of us, to picture Him hanging on the cross while I broke my Doritos chip and opened the coconut water container. I saw Him. I saw Him nailed to the cross. His marred form and shockingly bloody appearance made me gasp. He did not look like a man. He did not appear human.

I looked again—more closely than before. This time, I peered much deeper and with greater intensity. Our eyes met, and His gaze was irresistible. I found it difficult to continue staring into His eyes because they became overwhelming, yet at the same time, neither could I look away.

His eyes were beyond description. There are no words to articulate what I experienced. The love and peace I encountered could never be bought, prescribed, or conjured. Tears flowed from my eyes, choking my ability to speak. I could only silently mouth, "Thank You. I love You."

This encounter birthed this book.

HOW TO READ *HOLY COVENANT*

My first book, ***Holy Pillow Talk,*** is a prequel to ***Holy Covenant.*** In it, readers are encouraged to read the prayers and decrees aloud. It is crafted as an intimate dialogue between Jesus, your Bridegroom, and you, His beloved and cherished Bride. He speaks directly to you; you answer Him with pure devotion, deep worship, and intimate affection.

As you embark on this 30-day journey through ***Holy Covenant***, I kindly exhort you again to engage in this audible dialogue between you and your Beloved. Elohim is the Hebrew Name for God, and Adonai is the Hebrew Name for Lord. Throughout this book, you will call on a different name of God each day (e.g., Adonai Jireh, Elohim Shomri, etc.), corresponding to the day's focus. Doing this will reveal another layer of His promises, character, and wonder. You may or may not be familiar with some of His Names. Do not be intimidated with pronouncing them. Your perfection is not expected, just your effort.

This act of vocalizing these truths is a passionate connection, reminding us of His sacrifice while declaring the victory He purchased for us. When we audibly decree the Rhema (the spoken word of God) infused with the Logos (the written word of God), our spirit excels to another level of faith, and we know that faith comes by hearing His Word.

This book is a compilation of my unique studies, which identify the numerous blessings associated with observing Passover, communion, or the breaking of bread, along with my personal prayers and specific decrees. Multiple versions of Scripture have been used to capture and convey the intensity and depth of His sacrifice for us.

You will find a QR code at the end of each day's devotion. Please scan this with your phone or visit the website, www.amandahill.org, to listen to the corresponding song about Jesus, our Passover Lamb. The songs are essential to the day's devotion and have been carefully selected from various Christian genres, including praise/worship, Southern gospel, Latino, church hymns, and Black gospel. Finally, a section entitled "Taste and See" contains reflective questions to help you in your 30-day journey of remembering, discerning, and receiving what He has done for you.

Before you begin, let us recap what your devotion time might look like.

What do you need?

1. Bible
2. ***Holy Covenant*** book
3. Pen/Pencil
4. Communion elements
5. Phone (or another way to access the internet to play the song associated with the day)

What does the flow of each day look like?

1. Begin by reading the Scriptures at the top of the page.
2. Read aloud the prayers and decrees.
3. In your own words, take a moment to repent before the Lord for anything that might have grieved His heart.
4. Prepare the communion elements.
5. Scan the QR code or go to www.amandahill.org.
6. Click on the corresponding day.
7. As the song plays, partake of the communion elements, sing along, worship, and meditate on His sacrifice.
8. Read and answer the "Taste and See" questions for further revelation.

Finally, before you begin, I invite you to pray the following prayer.

Father, thank You for sending Your Son as the atoning sacrifice for my sins. Jesus, thank You for advocating with the Father by bearing my sins in Your Body on the tree. Holy Spirit, thank You for revealing the hidden mysteries and deeper depths of Jesus's tortured Body and shed Blood.

I receive this 30-day journey as an invitation to change my paradigm from observing Your sacrifice as an obligation, ritual, or tradition. Instead, it is a wooing call from You, my Bridegroom, to know Your love and sacrifice for me in a more intimate way. Whatever you have in store for me, I will say yes without hesitation or needing all the details first.

I am one who eats Your Flesh and drinks Your Blood because I believe in You and accept You as my Savior and Lord. Your Flesh is true spiritual food, and Your Blood is true spiritual drink. Your words are spirit and life; I embrace them fully. You are in me, and I am in You.

By faith, I receive the glorious blessings You provide as I observe **Your Holy Covenant** with me. I will remember Your death, burial, resurrection, and ascension until You come again. Each time I partake of Your Body and Blood, I prophesy to the kingdom of darkness that You are the King Who disarmed its authority and triumphantly defeated it through the cross!

As I meditate on Your bruised Body and shed Blood, I welcome the spiritual transaction, this holy impartation that takes place as I am infused with Your Body and transfused with Your Blood. I have been made complete in and through You.

Through Your Name, I will triumphantly wage war with Your Body and Blood, and I will see my life, my family's lives, Your Church, and my nation experience supernatural breakthrough. May the Lamb that was slain receive the full reward of His suffering! Amen!

DAY 1

PROTECTION

EXODUS 12:23-30

ELOHIM SHOMRI, God My Protector

I SPEAK

Thank You, Jesus, for Your sacrifice. I remember and meditate on the price You paid for me. The New Covenant, purchased by Your Body and Blood, serves as my weapon for warring triumphantly. In humility, I confess my sins and ask for Your forgiveness. In Your mercy, cleanse my heart, mind, words, behavior, and anything that contradicts Your character and Holy Spirit. Acquit me of my unconscious, unintended faults. According to the greatness of Your compassion, blot out my transgressions. Wash me thoroughly from my wickedness, guilt, and iniquity.

I receive Your promise of protection
through Your Body and Blood!

Protection is my portion, for You are Elohim Shomri, God my Protector. Just as You judged the gods of Egypt with Your mighty hand, so You also spared and protected Your people, Israel, with that same hand. Like Israel, my family is called by Your name—we are Your people. I decree that as for me and my house, we will steadfastly serve You and obey Your Word. Thank You that You judge every false god, but You protect us!

I apply the Blood of Jesus, the sinless Passover Lamb to every entrance, window, and door of my home. Therefore, I thank You that destruction will not touch my family or me. The enemy shall not harm us. The devourer must pass over and may not touch what concerns us.

As we dwell in Your shelter, O Most High, I declare we are stable, grounded, and entirely at rest under Your shadow. No enemy can withstand Your power!

Your Presence is our secret place.

I proclaim to You, Eternal One, that You are our refuge, our mighty fortress, and our God. There is no other god beside You. Who can compare? Who would even dare?

We lean into, rely on, and place all our trust in You, and as a result, we are secure. You rescue us from hidden traps, deadly hazards, and demonic plagues set by the enemy. Like a bird protecting its young, You cover us with Your feathers, protecting us under Your great, outstretched wings. Your truth and faithfulness form a shield around us, guarding us like a solid rock wall.

We are perfectly safe.

We will not fear the terrors that haunt the night, the enemy's arrows that fly during the day, or the evil plots and slanderous curses of the wicked. We will not fear the disease lurking in darkness or the disaster that wreaks havoc at noonday.

A thousand may fall at our side and ten thousand at our right hand, but these horrors will not come near us. Flooding, tornadoes, droughts, wildfires, hurricanes, earthquakes, hail, heat waves, cyclones, avalanches, landslides, tsunamis, blizzards, mudslides, or volcanic eruptions may not come near our home or my family. We will remain untouched, unharmed, and unaffected by death, destruction, and danger. We will only be spectators as we witness the punishment of divine repayment that awaits the wicked. Because of Your sacrifice, we will not suffer these things because we have been set securely on an inaccessibly high place, away from the enemy. We dwell in Your secret place. The enemy may see us, but neither he nor his dark kingdom can touch us.

Because we have made You our refuge, and You, Elohim Shomri, are our only home, no evil can even get close to us. Destruction, plagues, calamity, premature death, accidents, injuries, and tragedies will turn away at our door because of the Blood of Your Son, the spotless Lamb, Jesus Christ, the Messiah.

You command Your heavenly messengers to guard, accompany, defend, preserve, and keep us safe in every way. They will hold us up in their hands so we will not crash, stumble, fall, or even graze our foot on a stone. We will walk on lions and trample serpents under our feet.

Because we cling to and love You, Everlasting Father, You rescue us from harm, deliver us from trouble, and set us above danger. Because we know and understand the power in Your Name, we call on You, and

You answer us. We have a personal knowledge of Your mercy, love, and kindness.

We fully trust and rely on You, knowing You will never forsake us. Absolutely never.

You are with us through challenging times and trouble. You rescue and honor us. You reward us with many good years on this earth and allow us to witness Your salvation.

As one who is in covenant with You, I release a blessing on my family: my children, grandchildren, great-grandchildren, and those yet to be born.

I speak a generational blessing of protection over all future descendants. May the Lord bless, keep, protect, sustain, and guard you. May His glorious and gracious face shine upon you, enlighten and fill you with kindness, mercy, and favor. May the Lord lift His countenance of approval upon you, granting you peace and hope. May you know, experience, love, and serve Jesus all the days of your long, blessed, righteous life.

As I meditate on and gratefully eat Your Flesh and drink Your Blood, I abide in You and You in me. I remember and honor Your selfless sacrifice by observing communion.

Triumphantly, I claim, receive, and apply the blessing of protection for my life and my family's lives because that is what You paid for. May You receive the reward of Your suffering, my King. With thanks, joy, and faith, I appropriate Your disfigured Body and sacrificial Blood. I love You. Thank You, Jesus, for **Our Holy Covenant**.

ELOHIM SHOMRI RESPONDS

I am the God Who judged and then executed judgment on all the gods of Egypt, exhibiting their worthlessness and exalting My sovereignty. I am the Lord, the One true God. I am the head over all rulers and authorities, both on Earth and in Heaven. I purposefully made a public spectacle of all the powers and principalities of darkness. I disarmed the supernatural forces of evil that operate against you. I stripped them of their weapons and spiritual authority to accuse you. I triumphed over them through the cross, making them My prisoner.

Since they are My prisoners, they are also yours.

I have conquered death, Hell, and the grave, rendering them powerless and ineffective against you. I am your only true protection. I guard and guide you, ensuring that your foot does not slip. I am the One Who keeps you, and I do not slumber or sleep. I have never stopped watching over you. Trust in My unwavering, unfailing commitment to keep you safe. I am your shelter, protecting you from all danger, both day and night. I will shield you from every form of evil or calamity. I, Myself, guard you. You will be safe when you leave home, and I will ensure you return without harm. I protected you then, I protect you now, and I will protect you forevermore. So, do not give in to fear, for I am always near. Keep your gaze on Me, for I am faithful to infuse you with strength and provide help.

Now, advance forward and enforce My triumph, which My Body and Blood purchased for you. My sacrifice on the cross secured everything you need.

I am Elohim Shomri, God Your Protector. This is your inheritance from Me. I will protect you. This is My promise to you sealed by **Our Holy Covenant**.

Scripture references—Isaiah 41, Isaiah 43, Joshua 24, Psalm 19, Psalm 51, Psalm 59, Psalm 91, Psalm 121, Exodus 12, Colossians 2, John 6

Visit www.amandahill.org or scan the QR code below. Partake of the elements and then listen to the worship song that coincides with Day #1.

TASTE AND SEE

Review Psalm 91 and Psalm 121. Write down the promises from the Lord contained in these Scriptures that ensure our protection. His Word is true and does not lie, but our feelings and experiences can sometimes lead us astray.

Have there been moments or seasons when you felt you and/or your family were unprotected by the Lord? Did it seem as if the enemy came in and did whatever he wanted? If so, take a moment to recall and talk with the Father about this. Take a few moments and release any disappointment you may have.

DAY 2

REST

EXODUS 31:12-17, EXODUS 20:8-11

ADON HASHABBAT, Lord of the Sabbath

I OPEN

Thank You, Jesus, for Your sacrifice. I remember and meditate on the price You paid for me. The New Covenant, purchased by Your Body and Blood, serves as my weapon for warring triumphantly. In humility, I confess my sins and ask for Your forgiveness. In Your mercy, cleanse my heart, mind, words, behavior, and anything that contradicts Your character and Holy Spirit. Acquit me of my unconscious, unintended faults. According to the greatness of Your compassion, blot out my transgressions. Wash me thoroughly from my wickedness, guilt, and iniquity.

I receive Your promise of rest
through Your Body and Blood!

You are Adon HaShabbat, the Lord of the Sabbath, the Lord of rest. When I choose to rest in You, I find true peace. Burnout is not my destiny; Your peaceful rest is my inheritance.

I repent for striving, trying to earn Your grace and favor. I repent for the times that I have ignored Your command to rest. Forgive me. I obey You regarding every other command except taking a day to rest. Following Your instruction to rest, rejuvenates and resets my life and syncs me with You.

I admit that I do not know how to rest in the way You desire. Please teach me to rest, to truly rest.

Help me discover what my body needs as I embrace physical rest and rejuvenation, and release tension, stress, fatigue, and anxiety. Guide me in nurturing my spirit, welcoming quiet moments where Your Presence restores me. Show me how to care for my emotions, reclining in Your embrace where I can be vulnerable, heal, and become whole.

Light the path so I can encounter a mental respite, where my to-do lists, frustrations, and mental fog all become silent, bowing to Your Name. Help me focus on my needs and engage in self-care, which fuels my creative spirit in ways that bring joy and inspiration. Lead me to pathways where I can reset socially, setting boundaries where appropriate and cultivating rightly aligned, godly relationships as You see fit. Teach me how to refresh my senses, unplugging fully from the overload and letting me just be still.

Reset, refuel, and restore me to real rest.

I recognize the importance of rest, just as You rested from Your work. Therefore, I commit to taking one day each week to rest from my responsibilities. I will enjoy the life You have given me and refuse to become so busy that I neglect my blessings.

I resist anxiety, worry, and the snare of being pulled in different directions, spinning my wheels with busyness. I am determined to lead a productive, successful, fulfilling life rather than one filled with mere activity for the sake of being busy. Guard my heart so that I never wear busyness as a badge.

Every day of my life will be saturated with prayer, and I will offer You my requests with overflowing gratitude and thanksgiving. Your Name is Wonderful Counselor, Mighty God, Everlasting Father, the Prince of Peace. Your peace is real and wonderful. It transcends human understanding and reassures my heart; that peace stands guard over my heart and my mind.

I receive the gift of rest as I triumphantly war from a place of peaceful rest. Thank You for the rest You give to me on every side. It is my promise from You because we have cut covenant with one another. As I rest in You, none of my enemies can stand before me, for You hand them over to me.

Your rest is my weapon.

As I meditate on and gratefully eat Your Flesh and drink Your Blood, I abide in You and You in me. I remember and honor Your selfless sacrifice by observing communion.

Triumphantly, I claim, receive, and apply the blessing of rest in my life because that is what You paid for. May You receive the reward of Your suffering, my King. With thanks, joy, and faith, I appropriate Your pierced Body and righteous Blood. I love You. Thank You, Jesus, for **Our Holy Covenant**.

ADON HASHABBAT DECLARES

Are you feeling weary? Are you carrying a heavy burden? Come to Me, and I will gladly and graciously give you rest. Through **Our Holy Covenant**, your life is united with Mine; we are One. Take a deep breath and lean into and embrace My rest. Lean into Me.

Come away with Me, and you will regain and recover your life, your real life, not the counterfeit life you have been attempting to live.

Let Me show you how to experience an authentic Sabbath rest. I am Adon HaShabbat, the Lord of the Sabbath. As you walk with Me, work with Me, and watch Me, you will learn the unforced rhythms of My grace. I am gentle, humble, and easy to please, and I will never place anything heavy upon you. You will find refreshment and rest in Me.

Keep company with Me. Stay close to Me, and I will teach you how to live freely and lightly. Everything I ask of you will be pleasant and easy to bear.

Now, advance forward and enforce My triumph, which My Body and Blood purchased for you. My sacrifice on the cross secured everything you need.

I am Adon HaShabbat, the Lord of the Sabbath, the Lord Who gives you rest. This is your inheritance from Me. I will give you rest. This is My promise to you sealed by **Our Holy Covenant**.

Scripture references—Matthew 11, Joshua 21, 2 Chronicles 14, Isaiah 9, Hebrews 4, John 6

Visit www.amandahill.org or scan the QR code below. Partake of the elements and then listen to the worship song that coincides with Day #2.

TASTE AND SEE

Do you take one day a week to rest? If yes, do you find it challenging to do so? Recall the benefits of rest you have experienced. If you do not take one day to rest, what is preventing you?

Is your life filled with busyness and spinning wheels or with productive activities and fulfilling people? Evaluate your schedule with the Lord and ask Him what should be eliminated and what should remain.

DAY 3

EMOTIONAL HEALING

EXODUS 15:26, EXODUS 23:25

ADONAI ROPHE NEPHISH,
The Lord Who Heals My Soul

ADONAI ROPHE NEPHISH BEGINS

I willingly suffered for you. I carried your sins in My Body on the cross so that you would be dead to sin and live for righteousness. From My wounding flowed your healing. It is My gift to you.

My utter anguish and bursting chest healed your broken heart and emotions.

I restored you to wholeness, never-ending hope, and inexpressible joy. I am faithful to clean and bandage your wounds. I am the God of all comfort and will bring solace to you in the midst of your hurt. My sacrifice defeated despair, hopelessness, sadness, depression, discouragement, and all other ungodly emotions.

I was severely beaten and bruised. I bled internally and externally. The abuse I endured ripped Me open. Blood flowed from My neck, shoulders, and back. When the crowds saw Me, they were horrified. My face was so disfigured that I hardly looked human.

I was despised and rejected—a man of deep sorrows, intimately acquainted with suffering. Everyone was disgusted by Me and turned their backs on Me. Yet, I bore your weaknesses and grief. I willingly carried your sorrows and endured the torment of your sufferings. Why?

Because I love you.

Receive your healing from Me like you received your salvation from Me. Agree to this glorious exchange. Give Me your wounded soul, broken heart, and painful emotions, and receive My healed soul, perfect heart, and healthy emotions.

I am the God Who turns the bitter into sweet. I transformed the water during the Exodus; I can indeed do it with your emotions. Would you choose to trust Me? I can calm the whirlwind of unruly emotions and bring them into the right balance. I am the God Who heals your deep trauma. Let Me rewire your soul so that My Spirit leads you, not your emotions. Submit to My identity for and within you.

I fearfully and wonderfully created your emotional health.
I want to heal it, back to its original intent and design.

Now, advance forward and enforce My triumph, which My Body and Blood purchased for you. My sacrifice on the cross secured everything you need.

I am Adonai Rophe Nephish, the Lord Who Heals Your Soul. This is your inheritance from Me. You are healed. This is My promise to you sealed by **Our Holy Covenant**.

I RESPOND

Thank You, Jesus, for Your sacrifice. I remember and meditate on the price You paid for me. The New Covenant, purchased by Your Body and Blood, serves as my weapon for warring triumphantly. In humility, I confess my sins and ask for Your forgiveness. In Your mercy, cleanse my heart, mind, words, behavior, and anything that contradicts Your character and Holy Spirit. Acquit me of my unconscious, unintended faults. According to the greatness of Your compassion, blot out my transgressions. Wash me thoroughly from my wickedness, guilt, and iniquity.

I receive Your promise of emotional healing and wholeness through Your Body and Blood!

You are Adonai Rophe Nephish, the Lord Who Heals My Soul. I belong to You. You created every part of me and know my struggles, showing deep compassion and care for me.

I repent for the sins of the generations who have gone before me. Father, apply the Blood of Your beloved Son, Jesus, to the transgressions and iniquities of my ancestors. I repent on their behalf. Any of their or my sins that opened the door to imbue my emotions with brokenness and my heart with sickness, wash and forgive them and me, Lord.

Jesus, in Your justice, powerfully resolve the conflicts in me. Deal with my trust issues! Deal with my disappointment! Deal with my unbelief! Deal with my hope deferred! Deal with all negativity and every emotional fragmentation, blockage, and baggage.

Examine me for generational sins and iniquities, ungodly beliefs, familiar spirits, and unresolved traumas that keep me from You. None of these are too difficult for Your love. I want Your reign in me to be absolute, so I slow down to truly explore my heart with You. I know complete freedom in these areas is my birthright, so please do whatever You must to establish me in Your freedom. Do whatever it takes to restore my alignment to You.

I am willing to do my part, and I know You are faithful to do Yours.

I repent for aligning myself with any spirit other than Holy Spirit. I repent for agreeing with my fickle emotions and letting them rule over me. I repent for the places and decisions where I departed from Your Presence. I renounce my agreement with every generational sin, ungodly belief, toxic thought, wicked stronghold, and unhealthy emotion. I dismantle them in Your Truth. I revoke their ability to impact or influence my spirit, soul, and body any further. By the power of Your Name, I break the soul ties I have made with corrupted emotions, and I forbid them to operate in my life from this day forward. I dismantle and destroy the soul ties I have made with people, places, and possessions that have led me away from You. I cancel their influence on any facet of my life.

Heal all the traumatic, tormenting memories of my past.

I open myself to let go of unforgiveness and bitterness, and to relearn the thoughts of wholeness. I forgive those who have sinned against me and those who influenced me to sin. I forgive those who have used me and abused me. I release them for what they have done to me or said about me. I also forgive myself now in Your powerful Name, Jesus.

The same grace I extend to others, I receive for myself.

I renounce and revoke the enemy's legal rights in my life. The Blood of Jesus has been applied, and now, Satan, I command you to release your hold and flee from me now!

I ask for and command these demons, demonic oppressions, negative emotions, and their roots, stems, and seeds to be exposed and uprooted from my soul now, never to return. In Your Name, Jesus:

Abandonment, Rejection, Self-Pity, Victim, Competition, Jealousy, Striving, Isolation, Masturbation, Loneliness, Anger, Hatred, Rage, Resentment, Tantrums, Control, Denial, Domineering, Homosexuality, Fortune Telling, Levitation, Sorcery, Lesbianism, Pornography, Manipulation, Premarital Sex, Possessiveness, Voodoo, Sexual Sins, Witchcraft, Selfishness, Frigidity, Anxiety, False Responsibility, Fatigue, Nervousness, Restlessness, Weariness, Worry, Failure, Fears,

Burden, Dread, Intimidation, Paranoia, Oversensitivity, Worry, Greed, Deception, Confusion, Lying, Bitterness, Accusation, Blaming, Financial Bondage, Molestation, Complaining, Fault Finding, Gossip, New Age, Religious Spirits, Liberalism, Seduction, Antichrist, Judging, Ridicule, Unforgiveness, Depression, Adultery, Rape, Despair, Greed, Discouragement, Appeasement, Hopelessness, Insomnia, Oversleeping, Withdrawal, Bound Emotions, Escapism, Stealing, Forgetfulness, Laziness, Lethargy, Passivity, Self-Sabotage, Procrastination, Grief, Loss, Sadness, Sorrow, Pride, Heartbreak, Poverty, Occult, Arrogance, Vanity, Rebellion, Lust, Incest, Disobedience, Independence, Lying, Stubbornness, Condemnation, Guilt, Inferiority, Shame, Strife, Arguing, Contention, Fighting, Mocking, Trauma, Accidents, Shock, Violence, Abuse, Demonic Sex, Neglect, Envy, Unworthiness, Unbelief, Doubt, Inadequacy, Insecurity, Self-Hate, Helplessness, Hopelessness, Mistrust, Retaliation, Obsessiveness, Illegitimacy, Suspicion, Enabling, and any other negative emotion, GO!

Holy Spirit, replace these destructive emotions and demonic oppression with godly beliefs and Your infilling.

In Christ, I declare:

I am wanted.
I am secure.
I am whole.
I am courageous.
I am salt.
I am light.
I am forgiving.
I am righteous.
I am joyful.
I am steadfast.
I am discerning.
I am free.
I am loved.
I am strong.
I am confident.
I am healed.
I am heard.
I am hopeful.
I am redeemed.
I am resourceful.
I am peaceful.
I am focused.
I am important.
I am humble.
I am kind.
I am virtuous.
I am blessed.
I am known.
I am worthy.
I am truthful.

I am just.
I am bold.
I am intelligent.
I am self-controlled.
I am wise.
I am honest.
I am not alone.
I am compassionate.
I am gifted.
I am generous.
I am resilient.
I am seen.
I am perceptive.
I am content.
I am patient.
I am rested.
I am enough.
I am pure.
I am forgiven.

I am important to You, Jesus.

Even the seemingly small matters of my life are important to You; You have even numbered the very hairs on my head. Thank You for Your attention to every facet of my life. This truth brings me great comfort.

You are the God of all comfort, my very present help in my time of need, an ultimate source of consolation, strength, and support, especially during suffering, loss, and distress. You comfort and encourage me in every trouble, so I can also comfort and encourage those facing similar challenges with the same comfort I have received from You.

I desire to succeed, prosper, and maintain good health, just as my soul also prospers.

There is nothing I have faced, am facing, or might face that You have not already encountered. You sympathize with me in my weaknesses and fully understand me. Thank You. Jesus, my magnificent King-Priest, You were tempted in every way just as I am now, and You overcame it all.

You are the restorer, the reviver of my soul. When I am weak, You are strong. You give strength to the weary and increase power to those who feel powerless.

You are my wound Restorer,
heart Repairer, and emotion Healer.

Today I choose to take off the garment of heaviness and put on the garment of praise! Mourning and grief are not my portion, joy and strength are!

As I meditate on and gratefully eat Your Flesh and drink Your Blood, I abide in You and You in me. I remember and honor Your selfless sacrifice by observing communion.

Triumphantly, I claim, receive, and apply the blessing of emotional healing and wholeness in my life because that is what You paid for. May You receive the reward of Your suffering, my King. With thanks, joy, and faith, I appropriate Your bruised Body and hallowed Blood. I love You. Thank You, Jesus, for **Our Holy Covenant**.

Scripture references—Matthew 10, 2 Corinthians 1, 3 John, Psalm 46, Hebrews 4, 1 Peter 2, Isaiah 53, Psalm 23, Isaiah 40, Psalm 147, John 6

Visit www.amandahill.org or scan the QR code below. Partake of the elements and then listen to the worship song that coincides with Day #3.

TASTE AND SEE

Do you have a particular negative emotion that you find yourself struggling with repeatedly? Write it down here. Share your struggle with a friend or accountability partner and ask them to agree with you in prayer that this negative emotion and its roots are removed and will never be produced again in your life.

Look at the "I am" list and read it again out loud.

DAY 4

FAVOR

EXODUS 3:21, EXODUS 12:36, ACTS 2:47

ELOHIM CHEN, God of Grace (Favor)

I INITIATE

Thank You, Jesus, for Your sacrifice. I remember and meditate on the price You paid for me. The New Covenant, purchased by Your Body and Blood, serves as my weapon for warring triumphantly. In humility, I confess my sins and ask for Your forgiveness. In Your mercy, cleanse my heart, mind, words, behavior, and anything that contradicts Your character and Holy Spirit. Acquit me of my unconscious, unintended faults. According to the greatness of Your compassion, blot out my transgressions. Wash me thoroughly from my wickedness, guilt, and iniquity.

I receive Your promise of grace and favor in my life through Your Body and Blood!

I appreciate what Your suffering has purchased and provided for me. Favor is a tremendous blessing of Our covenant. The world is jealous of the unearned favor granted to me because it is the same favor that was bestowed upon You. This extraordinary blessing came at a tremendous cost to You, yet You selflessly extended it to me, and my heart overflows with gratitude. Jesus, Your sacrifice purchased my favor, the kind of favor that is not fair. I could never earn it. I do not deserve it, but you offer it just the same, and I wholeheartedly receive it!

Silver and gold pale in comparison to the magnificent grace You have lavishly poured out on me. Thank You for the abundant blessings You shower upon my life, for I stand as the righteousness of God in Christ Jesus. Your favor envelops me, offering protection under Your magnificent canopy of kindness and unspeakable joy.

You have designed me to overflow with influence. I am Your favored influencer! As I reflect Your character and example, I hold the plumbline of truth and holiness. You have enriched my life with Your divine favor because I abide in You, Jesus, and You abide in me. I am increasing in wisdom and stature and favor with the Father and with others. Your favor shines brightly and brilliantly upon my life.

Holy Spirit, align me with the right people, in the right place, and at the right time.

I reject any doors, relationships, or opportunities that are not orchestrated by You. Sharpen my discernment for those whose hearts are filled with opportunism, usury, and self-promotion. Let true motives be revealed, guarding me from flattery, which leads to snares of destruction.

Thank You for trusting me to walk into rooms, sit at tables, and stand on platforms far greater than I imagined. You are truly Elohim Chen, the God of boundless grace and unmerited favor. As You expand my sphere of influence and grant me greater authority over my territory, I embrace a spirit of humility and honor. I will not hoard my influence, contacts, or blessings. I reject false humility, workaholism, pride, competition, dishonor, jealousy, self-reliance, envy, and greed. Let me crave Your Presence and not a promotion.

May I seek Your face and not Your hands.

I desire to hunger and thirst for You and nothing more. You are the One Who satisfies me. You are more than enough, Lord. When I have You, I have all that I need.

I will cling to integrity. I vow to be the same person in private as I am in the spotlight. I decree that success will not change who You have created me to be.

Love is the most excellent way. Love is kind and thoughtful, bears all things, and believes the best in and of others. It is not envious, arrogant, rude, overly sensitive, easily angered, or self-seeking. Therefore, I choose love.

I will prefer my brother and sister, championing and cheering them on as they advance. I reject selfishness, selfish ambition, control, manipulation, and opportunism. Let my motives be pure, holy, and righteous.

Holy Spirit, purify my heart.

The gift You have placed inside me makes room for me and escorts me before great, influential people. I will not waste or squander it. I will steward what You have entrusted to me. It all belongs to You. You are the source.

Father, Your favor shines upon me because of Your Son, Jesus. Therefore, I ask You to affirm and bless the work of my hands—yes, confirm and prosper the labor of my hands, Lord.

The fountain of life flows within me because I have discovered wisdom, the key to growing in Your delight and favor. Your favor is far better than silver or gold; it surrounds me like a shield, protecting me from my enemies.

As I meditate on and gratefully eat Your Flesh and drink Your Blood, I abide in You and You in me. I remember and honor Your selfless sacrifice by observing communion.

Triumphantly, I claim, receive, and apply the blessing of boundless grace and unmerited favor in my life because that is what You paid for. May You receive the reward of Your suffering, my King. With thanks, joy, and faith, I appropriate Your pierced Body and precious Blood. I love You. Thank You, Jesus, for **Our Holy Covenant**.

ELOHIM CHEN DECLARES

I created you to carry My favor and designed you to be one of a kind. You are unique, and your distinction sets you apart. I do not want you to be like anyone else.

I love you—so be *you!*

My joy in you is contagious! The anointing on your life attracts people who want to serve, give, and work alongside you. My favor on you will draw people of greater influence into your life.

Get ready, for I am increasing your capacity. While it will feel uncomfortable initially, I must enlarge, stretch, and lengthen you to contain this new level of increase. I long to give you more.

Others favor you because you are full of strategy, wisdom, counsel, revelation, and resources. My anointing on your life will cause your influence to multiply exponentially.

I have created you to be the salt of the earth and the light of the world. I have anointed you to be a positive influence, a moral compass, and a voice of truth. I will guard and protect you as you represent Me.

I am the God Who opens doors that no man can shut, and I shut doors that no man can open. You have been faithful, and your humility has delighted Me. I am going to send you to places you have never even asked for, all because I can trust you. So, get ready for new keys: keys of authority, influence, multiplication, resources, and access.

I am extending My scepter and declare, "Favor granted!"

My Blood-stained palms broke the curse from your hands, ensuring your success in everything you touch.

Now, advance forward and enforce My triumph, which My Body and Blood purchased for you. My sacrifice on the cross secured everything you need.

I am Elohim Chen, the God of Grace and Favor, Who floods you with favor because you are My favorite! This is your inheritance from Me. I will favor you. This is My promise to you sealed by **Our Holy Covenant**.

Scripture references—Proverbs 6, Joel 2, Proverbs 3, Psalm 5, 2 Corinthians 5, Psalm 90, Proverbs 8, Proverbs 22, Proverbs 18, Isaiah 54, Matthew 5, Luke 14, Numbers 6, Isaiah 22, 1 Corinthians 13, Psalm 107, John 6

Visit www.amandahill.org or scan the QR code below. Partake of the elements and then listen to the worship song that coincides with Day #4.

TASTE AND SEE

Many times, His favor on you will provoke others to jealousy. Have you ever encountered this from people who you thought would champion you? If so, what happened?

Did this experience cause you to shrink back from moving forward and confidently carrying His favor in your life? Did it make you angry and bitter, striving to compete instead of shaking off the bite of their envy? Or did you respond with the character of Christ, shaking off their offense? Take a moment to assess your possible heart wound and discuss it with Holy Spirit.

DAY 5

CONFIDENCE AND COURAGE

EXODUS 14:8, 13; NUMBERS 33:3-4

ADONAI OMETZ-LEVI, The Lord My Courage

I BEGIN

Thank You, Jesus, for Your sacrifice. I remember and meditate on the price You paid for me. The New Covenant, purchased by Your Body and Blood, serves as my weapon for warring triumphantly. In humility, I confess my sins and ask for Your forgiveness. In Your mercy, cleanse my heart, mind, words, behavior, and anything that contradicts Your character and Holy Spirit. Acquit me of my unconscious, unintended faults. According to the greatness of Your compassion, blot out my transgressions. Wash me thoroughly from my wickedness, guilt, and iniquity.

I receive Your promise of steadfast confidence and outrageous courage in my life through Your Body and Blood!

You are my light and my salvation. Whom shall I fear? You are the refuge and fortress of my life. Whom shall I dread? My heart will not be afraid even if an army encamps against me. Even if war rises against me, I will remain confident. I will walk carefully, living life with honor, purpose, and courage. I will avoid those who tolerate and enable evil, not as the unwise but as the wise, making the most of my time on Earth.

One thing I ask of You, and that I will seek: Allow me to dwell in Your house all the days of my life, to gaze upon Your beauty. In times of trouble, You hide me in Your secret place. I wait for You and confidently expect Your help. I will be strong and let my heart take courage. Yes, I will wait for You, Lord, and I confidently trust Your promises.

You are the great High Priest Who understands and sympathizes with my weaknesses and temptations. You have faced every temptation, yet You have never sinned. It is a privilege to approach the throne of grace with confidence and without fear so that I may receive mercy for my shortcomings and failures. Here is where I find Your amazing grace to help me in my time of need.

I will not lose my confidence during difficulties, for it carries a glorious and great reward. Grant me patient endurance so that I will not compromise, even under challenging circumstances. I am confident that I can trust You, and You will see me through.

You are Adonai Ometz-Levi! I find all the courage I need in You!

I will be strong and courageous. I will not be afraid or worried, for You go before me. You are with me.

I will trust in You and rely on You with all my heart. I refuse to depend on my insight and understanding. In all my ways, I will acknowledge You, and You will make my path straight. My hope is in You, Lord. I have confidence in You, and I will act righteously. I dwell in the land and securely feed on Your faithfulness. I delight myself in You, for You give me the desires and petitions of my heart. I commit my way to You, and I trust in You, knowing You will act.

Your law will never depart from my mouth, but I will meditate on it day and night so that I may be careful to do everything written. Then I will be prosperous and successful. I will not be afraid or intimidated. I will be confident and courageous.

I declare that I have extraordinary confidence and boldness before You, Lord. If I ask anything according to Your purpose, You will hear me. I know for sure that You hear me and listen to me in whatever I ask, and because of this, I know I have received what I ask of You. Thank You for hearing me.

As I meditate on and gratefully eat Your Flesh and drink Your Blood, I abide in You and You in me. I remember and honor Your selfless sacrifice by observing communion.

Triumphantly, I claim, receive, and apply the blessing of unbelievable confidence, and unstoppable courage in my life because that is what You paid for. May You receive the reward of Your suffering, my King. With thanks, joy, and faith, I appropriate Your beaten Body and perfect Blood. I love You. Thank You, Jesus, for **Our Holy Covenant**.

ADONAI OMETZ-LEVI RESPONDS

I did not give you a spirit of timidity, cowardice, or fear; instead, I gave you a spirit of power, love, sound judgment, and personal discipline.

I am revealing Myself to you. I want you to know Me and be personally acquainted with Me, so you will have absolute faith and assurance in Me and in the truth of My deity.

Be strong, confident, and empowered by the grace that is found only in Me. I am the only One Who assures your safety and instills pure reliance.

I am your confidence—firm and strong—and I will keep your foot from being caught in a snare.

Hear My command to you today: Be strong, confident, and courageous! Do everything I have commanded you. Never turn to the right or left so you will prosper and succeed wherever you go. My perfect peace calms you in every situation and gives you courage and strength for every challenge.

Now, advance forward and enforce My triumph, which My Body and Blood purchased for you. My sacrifice on the cross secured everything you need.

I am Adonai Ometz-Levi, the Lord Your Courage,
Who imparts to you confidence and courage.
This is your inheritance from Me. I will give you My
confidence and courage. This is My promise to you
sealed by **Our Holy Covenant.**

Scripture references—Psalm 27, Hebrews 4, Deuteronomy 31, 2 Timothy 1, Psalm 4, Proverbs 3, Psalm 37, Joshua 1, John 15, 1 John 5, John 6

Visit www.amandahill.org or scan the QR code below. Partake of the elements and then listen to the worship song that coincides with Day #5.

TASTE AND SEE

Have you ever been in a situation where distrust and fear spoke louder than confidence and courage? What steps did you take to combat those negative, ungodly voices?

Confidence and courage grow as we spend time in His Word, in worship, and in communing with Holy Spirit. These are His gifts to you that you obtain, not attain, and receive, not earn. Over the next several hours, thank Him for these blessings and embrace them with joy.

DAY 6

HARVEST

ACTS 2:37–47

ADON HAKATZIR, Lord of the Harvest

THE EKKLESIA INITIATES

Thank You, Jesus, for Your sacrifice. We remember and meditate on the price You paid for us, Your Bride. The New Covenant, purchased by Your Body and Blood, serves as our weapons for warring triumphantly. In humility, we confess the sins of Your Church and ask for Your forgiveness. In Your mercy, cleanse our hearts, minds, words, behaviors, and anything that contradicts Your character and Holy Spirit. Acquit us of our unconscious, unintended faults. According to the greatness of Your compassion, blot out our transgressions. Wash us thoroughly from our wickedness, transgressions, and iniquities.

We receive Your promise of harvest
through Your Body and Blood!

Adon HaKatzir, You are the Lord of the Harvest, and we ask You to stir the hearts of Your people with compassion for the lost. The harvest is ripe and plentiful; many need to hear about the good news of salvation, but the workers are few. Therefore, we ask You to send out workers into Your harvest fields, for they are white and ready.

The days of acceleration are no longer coming. They are here. They are now upon us. We are in the last days when the harvest will be so great that those plowing the fields will overtake those who are still reaping the harvest, and those treading the grapes will surpass those who are planting.

We set our faces like flint and petition You to pour out Your Spirit upon all flesh. We ask for conviction to flood the hearts of every person alive. When they hear the gospel of salvation, let Your sword of truth pierce their hearts. May they repent from their sinful ways, accept and follow You as Messiah, be baptized in Your Name, and receive the gift of Holy Spirit! We cry out for mercy, Lord! Remove the spiritual blinders of deception that keep people from seeing the truth of the gospel.

You desire that none would perish, but that all would come to repentance.

You are long-suffering, Adon HaKatzir. You are patient in withholding Your wrath. Your immense kindness leads us to repentance.

We, Your Ekklesia, ask You to release Your angels, the ministering spirits sent forth to minister to those who will inherit salvation. Father, send Your Spirit to draw them to Jesus!

We plead Your Blood over every neighborhood, county, city, and region. We release the light of Jesus to shine into every dark corner where sin is thriving. We bind rebellion, disobedience, lawlessness, addiction, and crime. We ask for exposure to fall upon cartels, mafia, gangs, traffickers, brothels, and every form of evil that holds people in bondage.

Jesus, we apply Your Blood for those deceived and bound by sexual perversion. We cry out for every person in or affiliated with the LGBTQ+ community. We command that the scales of delusion are falling off their eyes!

Holy Spirit, come and encounter every Muslim, Buddhist, Hindu, atheist, satanist, and agnostic with the overwhelming, passionate love of Jesus the Messiah.

Let Your holy, convicting Presence, and relentless love pour out on the campuses of every elementary, middle, and high school and all the universities in this land!

Invade the studios of Hollywood, the newsrooms of every media outlet, every government building, classroom, and business office. Shake everything that can be shaken!

Send the fire of Your Holy Spirit!

Lord of the Harvest, let the winds of Your Spirit blow from the north, south, east, and west. We say to the north, "Give them up!" And to the south, "Don't hold them back!" And we speak to the east, "Hand them over!" And to the west, "Let them go!"

We command the enemy to release the sons and daughters of our God. The Father demands them back, every last one who bears His Name. They were created for Your glory, Jesus! You breathed Your breath into each one of them.

Jesus, we appeal to Heaven for every prodigal who has been running away from Your conviction and Your call. We declare that the season of immoral, rebellious, and reckless living has ended. We send the power of the gospel through dreams and encounters with Jesus, ministering angels, holy witnesses, or any other avenue You see fit.

Shake whatever You need to shake, Holy Spirit! If necessary, let their finances dwindle, and let friends who once comforted them and participated in their sins turn against them, casting them overboard like Jonah. If it takes a storm to bring them back, let it rage! No matter where they are, they are never too far from Your Presence, so we ask that the fear of the Lord be released now! Whatever it takes, Lord. We remove our own will and desires. We let go of trying to control how You move in their lives. Just do whatever You need to do.

We declare that their senses, their right minds are returning to them. We sound the alarm and roar, "Wake up!" We call them back to Your House, Father. There is always room at Your table, Lord. Restoration is Your heart for every prodigal, so we call them home to You. We prophesy that celebrations are happening all across the earth as ones who were lost are now found, and once dead, they are now alive! Let the feasting, dancing, and music with overflowing joy and gratitude commence!

Let a mighty army of truth-loving, non-compromising,
Jesus-devoted, miracle-performing
witnesses arise in every nation.

We declare that the undiluted, unapologetic gospel of salvation is being preached, reaching every corner, territory, culture, people group, tribe, and tongue.

You are the Lord of the Harvest, the God Who saves! May every man, woman, boy, and girl encounter Your conviction and embrace the cross of Jesus, the Christ, turning from sin and receiving salvation!

As we meditate on and gratefully eat Your Flesh and drink Your Blood, we abide in You and You in us. We remember and honor Your selfless sacrifice by observing communion.

Triumphantly, we claim, receive, and apply the blessing of unprecedented harvest in Your Kingdom because that is what You paid for. May You receive the reward of Your suffering, our King. With thanks, joy, and faith, we appropriate Your torn Body and sacred Blood. We love You. Thank You, Jesus, for **Our Holy Covenant**

ADON HAKATZIR DECLARES

I extend an invitation of salvation to everyone. I do not delay, and I am not slow about My promises, but I am patient, not wishing for any to perish but for all to come to repentance. Just as all of Heaven rejoices when one sinner repents, so also My heart grieves when My offer of salvation is refused.

My Spirit beckons those who do not know Me to arise from spiritual slumber to new life! My glory and brilliance has risen. While darkness covers the earth, and deep darkness the people, do not fear, for I am rising!

Nations will see My light!

Whoever calls upon My Name will be saved. But how will they call on Me if they have not yet believed? And how can they believe in Me if they have not yet heard? And how can they hear My message of life without a preacher? And how will they preach unless they are commissioned and sent? How beautiful and delightful are the feet of those who bring the joyful good news, announcing peace and salvation!

I am releasing harvest mantles to wilderness voices and pure vessels. They will carry My gospel to the ends of the earth until all have heard!

Now, advance forward and enforce My triumph, which My Body and Blood purchased for you. My sacrifice on the cross secured everything you need.

I am Adon HaKatzir, the Lord of the Harvest! This is your inheritance from Me. I will give you the harvest of the ages. This is My promise to you sealed by **Our Holy Covenant.**

Scripture references—Matthew 9, John 4, Luke 10, Romans 1, Romans 2, 2 Peter 3, 1 Corinthians 15, Amos 9, 1 Corinthians 12, Hebrews 12, Isaiah 43, Isaiah 60, Romans 10, Isaiah 52, John 6, Luke 15

Visit www.amandahill.org or scan the QR code below. Partake of the elements and then listen to the worship song that coincides with Day #6.

TASTE AND SEE

Are you consistent in sharing your faith with others? If not, what holds you back? Do you feel embarrassed or unqualified?

Has the Lord placed a specific nation, people group, organization, or person in your spirit to intercede and pray for? If yes, who is it and what is your prayer strategy?

DAY 7

ANGELIC ASSISTANCE

EXODUS 14:19, JOSHUA 5:10–15, ACTS 12

ADONAI TZEVAOT, The Lord of Hosts

I SPEAK

Thank You, Jesus, for Your sacrifice. I remember and meditate on the price You paid for me. The New Covenant, purchased by Your Body and Blood, serves as my weapon for warring triumphantly. In humility, I confess my sins and ask for Your forgiveness. In Your mercy, cleanse my heart, mind, words, behavior, and anything that contradicts Your character and Holy Spirit. Acquit me of my unconscious, unintended faults. According to the greatness of Your compassion, blot out my transgressions. Wash me thoroughly from my wickedness, guilt, and iniquity.

I receive Your promise of angelic assistance and heavenly intervention in my life through Your Body and Blood!

Thank You, Father, for Your mighty army of angels, a celestial host ready to defend and support me. As I boldly declare Your Word, I trust that these divine warriors are being dispatched to operate, assist, and intervene on my behalf, weaving their strength and direction into my life. Holy Spirit, I ask for sharper discernment, a keen awareness, and an illumination of my spirit to recognize the angelic forces who work for me and alongside me. I prophesy a never-ending, surging increase in angelic activity around me and declare that all demonic activity is forbidden and shut down in Jesus's Name. I eagerly welcome Your angels to bring forth all I need and gently remove what no longer serves me.

In the mighty Name of Jesus, the crucified Savior Who conquered death and ascended to glory, I boldly command that all pathways to Hell be sealed shut. Let the divine floodgates of the Third Heaven swing wide above me, allowing an outpouring of all that Heaven has.

May the portals of holy angelic access burst forth now, bringing forth their unparalleled power and unwavering assistance regarding every aspect of my life.

Because of my covenant with You, through Your Body and Blood, angelic assistance, protection, guidance, and intervention is my portion. As Your fiery messengers descend and ascend back and forth through Your spiritual ladder, may they connect the Third Heaven to Earth, creating a connection of divine purpose and support for which they were created.

In the Name of Jesus, let the angels be released to fulfill the purpose for which they were created. Adonai Tzevaot, what a profound honor You have granted me as a human being, breathing Your life into me.

You fashioned me in Your Own likeness and image, granting me the authority to reign and have dominion.

In deep awe and reverence, I worship You, Jesus, not the beings You created. They are fellow servants, along with me. Thank You for sending Your angels like the winds and Your servants like flames of fire. I welcome and embrace every angel You have specifically assigned to assist me in my journey!

Mighty Adonai Tzevaot, I ask You to release and activate these, Your angel armies, valiant warriors from Heaven now, in Jesus's Name!

As I feel the shifting and swirling winds around me, I recognize that You have released Your holy warriors to assist me in advancing Your glorious Kingdom of Light. Send forth the Guardian Angels, Angels of Revelation, Harvest Angels, Angels of Fire, Healing Angels, Angels of Provision, Messenger Angels, Angels of Consecration, Worshipping Angels, Warrior Angels, Justice Angels, Angels of Prosperity, Dream Angels, Angels of Awakening, Destiny Angels, Angels of Justice, Government Angels, Angels of Deliverance, and any other angelic warriors that I may need.

As I meditate on and gratefully eat Your Flesh and drink Your Blood, I abide in You and You in me. I remember and honor Your selfless sacrifice by observing communion.

Triumphantly, I claim, receive, and apply the blessing of angelic assistance in my life because that is what You paid for. May You receive the reward of Your suffering, my King. With thanks, joy, and faith, I appropriate Your crushed Body and holy Blood. I love You. Thank You, Jesus, for **Our Holy Covenant.**

ADONAI TZEVAOT RESPONDS

Dear one, there are more angels working for you than there are demons working against you.

Assistance is available as soon as you ask—that is all you need to do! You have never been this way before, and you need angelic assistance to guide you through these uncharted territories. I am the Captain of the Host of Heaven, and My army is at your disposal; they are never defeated. The angel of the Lord struck down one hundred and eighty-five thousand soldiers in a single night. You have no idea how often My warriors have protected, defended, guided, provided for, strengthened, and comforted you.

There have even been times when I have instructed angels to delay you and stand in your way. Sometimes it was because you were out of time and on other occasions it was due to your choices, which displeased me. Either way, their presence was because I sent them.

At this history-defining time, you have stepped into a pivotal moment when I am releasing My messengers to orchestrate divine connections, tip the prayer bowls in Heaven, restore what was stolen, anoint you with a double portion of power, mantle you for a new season of purpose, shatter chains of confinement, ignite awakening fires, and so much more that I have preserved for this moment.

Now, advance forward and enforce My triumph, which My Body and Blood purchased for you. My sacrifice on the cross secured everything you need.

I am Adonai Tzevaot, the Lord of Hosts, Who dispatches My angel armies to serve you as you press ahead, expanding My glorious Kingdom. This is your inheritance from Me. I will send angels to assist you. This is My promise to you sealed by **Our Holy Covenant.**

Scripture references—Revelation 19, Revelation 22, Psalm 8, Joshua 5, Luke 1, Daniel 9, 2 Kings 19, Psalm 91, Exodus 23, Genesis 28, John 6, Joshua 3

Visit www.amandahill.org or scan the QR code below. Partake of the elements and then listen to the worship song that coincides with Day #7.

TASTE AND SEE

Have you ever had a situation where you knew an angel was present? If so, recall and record what happened.

Is there a specific area where you need angelic intervention right now? Ask Holy Spirit to dispatch assistance to you and your situation speedily. Remember to journal what happens in that circumstance to strengthen your faith.

DAY 8

UNDIGNIFIED PROPHETIC WORSHIP

EXODUS 15:1–21

EL SHADDAI, God Almighty

I OPEN

Thank You, Jesus, for Your sacrifice. I remember and meditate on the price You paid for me. The New Covenant, purchased by Your Body and Blood, serves as my weapon for warring triumphantly. In humility, I confess my sins and ask for Your forgiveness. In Your mercy, cleanse my heart, mind, words, behavior, and anything that contradicts Your character and Holy Spirit. Acquit me of my unconscious, unintended faults. According to the greatness of Your compassion, blot out my transgressions. Wash me thoroughly from my wickedness, guilt, and iniquity.

I receive Your promise of undignified prophetic worship in my life through Your Body and Blood!

When I meditate on Your sacrifice, Our covenant, and what You have done for me, how can I do anything less than offer my highest praise, my most undignified dance, and my loudest shout of triumph to You, El Shaddai, God Almighty!

Forgive me for the times when my worship has been lazy due to my lukewarm love and apathetic heart toward You.

I repent for not presenting a sacrifice of worship that would be acceptable. I repent for offering You something that costs me nothing. You gave everything for and to me; therefore, I vow to give You all my worship. My passionate, affectionate, intimate, and undignified praise is the least that I can do. I take pleasure in expressing my gratitude to You, my King! There is nothing and no one who compares with You. I love to lift You up.

All Your angels praise You. Your heavenly hosts cannot stop filling the earth with shouts of glory! The sun, moon, and stars all raise a cosmic chorus of thunderous worship to You! Every living being, from the smallest insects crawling on the land to the massive creatures swimming in the ocean's depths, echoes in their adoration to the King of all the earth!

I will sing a brand-new spontaneous song to You, expressing to everyone how wonderful You are. I gratefully and generously pour out my oil on Your feet in deep gratitude for what You paid on the cross for me. Like Miriam, I break forth with undignified dancing, making music, and singing Your praises to the rhythm of the timbrel and drums. I provoke others to join in without reservation. I am Your humble and faithful lover, and You adorn me with Your beauty as I triumph in Your glory.

My weapons of war bring vengeance on every spirit contrary to You, binding kings with chains and rulers with iron shackles.

When I extravagantly dance, the chains and restraints that the enemy has attempted to put on me get shifted, shackling and fettering him and his kingdom, creating a boomerang effect.

I am a praise-filled warrior, and my job is to enforce the judgment decreed against the enemies of Your Kingdom. I accept this assignment with joy and faith! I align with and belong to the tribe of Judah.

Just as David's dancing welcomed the Ark of the Covenant, so also my praise ushers in Your Presence. My sound is consecrated, not compromised. Therefore, I break open hard, resistant, demonic atmospheres with the clap of my hands, the stomp of my feet, and the shout from my mouth. My voice is a weapon, and I declare that my sound causes prison doors to shake, freeing captives from their bondage.

Every time I express my praise—whether by playing an instrument, shouting for joy, jumping, dancing, confessing Your goodness, kneeling or bowing in awe and submission, singing spontaneously, lifting my hands in thanksgiving, boasting about Your greatness, rejoicing with exceedingly boundless joy, or prostrating in reverence—I unlock a new level of authority to legislate in the spirit realm!

Your high and holy praises fill my mouth, and my shouted praises are my weapons of war!

Worthy and deserving is the Lamb that was sacrificed to receive power and riches and wisdom and might and honor and glory and blessing. To Him Who sits on the throne and to the Lamb be blessing and honor and glory and dominion forever and ever.

As I meditate on and gratefully eat Your Flesh and drink Your Blood, I abide in You and You in me. I remember and honor Your selfless sacrifice by observing communion.

Triumphantly, I claim, receive, and apply the blessing of undignified prophetic worship in my life because that is what You paid for. May You receive the reward of Your suffering, my King. With thanks, joy, and faith, I appropriate Your wounded Body and worthy Blood. I love You. Thank You, Jesus, for **Our Holy Covenant.**

EL SHADDAI DECREES

It is my greatest delight to give you victory. Oh, the immense joy I experience when you worship Me freely without restraint, heart unguarded, hands uplifted, eyes focused, with feet leaping. I see your heart, but I also want to see you demonstrate and express your love for Me through your worship. While others offer sleepy, half-hearted worship, your genuine sacrifice is what captures My attention. It is what I am drawn to.

Do you understand that when you worship out of simple obedience, even when you do not feel like it, it delights My heart? Let Me tell you what your worship births! Your high praise enforces My judgments against your enemies. Your shout makes impenetrable walls fall. Your new songs break old cycles. Your new sound shatters traumatic seasons. Your undignified dance produces joy. When you worship Me for Who I am, it moves Me. Thank you.

Now, advance forward and enforce My triumph, which My Body and Blood purchased for you. My sacrifice on the cross secured everything you need.

I am El Shaddai, God Almighty, Who imparts desire for undignified prophetic worship, which is My favorite! This is your inheritance from Me. Worship is your warfare. Praise is your weapon. I receive your authentic worship. This is My promise to you sealed by **Our Holy Covenant.**

Scripture references—Psalm 148, Psalm 149, Psalm 98, Psalm 144, Psalm 150, Isaiah 25, John 6, Revelation 5

Visit www.amandahill.org or scan the QR code below. Partake of the elements and then listen to the worship song that coincides with Day #8.

TASTE AND SEE

Have you ever exerted so much passion and energy during worship that you began to sweat? If so, how did you feel? What did you experience?

Regardless of whether you answered yes or no to question number 1, take a moment today to offer a deeper level of sacrificial praise. Begin by reading about how David danced before the Lord. Then, follow his example and do the same. Afterward, take some time to write down your experiences.

DAY 9

PHYSICAL HEALING

EXODUS 15:26, EXODUS 23:25

ADONAI RAPHA, The Lord Who Heals

I BEGIN

Thank You, Jesus, for Your sacrifice. I remember and meditate on the price You paid for me. The New Covenant, purchased by Your Body and Blood, serves as my weapon for warring triumphantly. In humility, I confess my sins and ask for Your forgiveness. In Your mercy, cleanse my heart, mind, words, behavior, and anything that contradicts Your character and Holy Spirit. Acquit me of my unconscious, unintended faults. According to the greatness of Your compassion, blot out my transgressions. Wash me thoroughly from my wickedness, guilt, and iniquity.

I receive Your promise of physical healing, health, and wholeness in my life through Your Body and Blood!

Jesus, You were tormented, reviled, insulted, and despised, all while You bore my sickness and carried my pain. Even so, You did not revile or insult in return. You did not sin, nor was any deceit or threats of vengeance found in Your mouth. Instead, You entrusted Yourself to the Father, carrying my sins in Your Body on the cross, willingly offering Yourself as a sacrifice on that altar for my well-being that I might die to sin and live for righteousness.

By Your Blood, I have been saved, and by Your wounds, I have been healed.

Thank You, Jesus, for purchasing my freedom and redeeming me from the curse of the law and its condemnation by becoming a curse for me. I agree with the promise that I am free and redeemed! I confess that because I am in You, the power of Your life-giving Spirit has set me free from the law of sin and death, which includes sickness and disease! Jesus, You did what the law could not do! You overcame sin and removed its penalty and power.

Jesus, You never turned away anyone who came to You for healing during Your time on Earth. You had compassion on the one, the few, and the multitudes. You healed them all. When the woman with the issue of blood touched the fringe of Your tallit, she was immediately healed of her suffering. You healed then, and You heal today because You are the God who does not change. So, I come to You now in faith, believing Your sacrifice has already healed me.

I will continually bless and affectionately praise You! All that is within me blesses Your holy Name. I will never forget any of Your benefits. You forgive all my sins and heal all my diseases. You redeem my life from the pit and crown me with loving-kindness and tender mercy. You satisfy my years with good things so that my youth is renewed like the eagle.

I submit my body to You, Holy Spirit.

My body is Your temple, Your dwelling place. I am not my own. I was bought with the price of Your beaten Body, Jesus. I was purchased with Your precious Blood, and You made me Your own. So then, I will honor and glorify You with my body.

I repent for the known and unknown sins of the generations who have gone before me. Father, apply the Blood of Your beloved Son, Jesus, to the transgressions and iniquities of my ancestors. I repent on their behalf. Any sin, theirs or mine, that opened the door to inflict diseases, disorders, sicknesses, and/or infirmities, wash and forgive them, Lord. I revoke and renounce the enemy's legal rights. I declare that all generational curses and familiar spirits affecting my physical health be reversed by the shed Blood of the Passover Lamb, transforming those generational curses into generational blessings!

Holy Spirit, help me to be careful and wise about what I eat and drink. Forgive me for the times I have been gluttonous and eaten poorly. I rebuke obesity from my life and bloodline. Jesus, help me to prioritize exercising on a regular basis. I want my body to last so that Your assignments and purposes in my life may be completed and fulfilled. All my ordained days are written in Your book. I confess that I will live them out in healing, health, and wholeness.

Father, thank You for using the medical industry to aid in healing. Thank You for the wisdom and compassion You have given to scientists, doctors, nurses, and all the healthcare workers. Thank You for using them as instruments of healing. However, I acknowledge that You are the One true Healer, not them and not big pharma. I rebuke the spirit of pharmakeia from my life, which seeks to replace You. You are the only One who heals.

I believe Your Word, Adonai Rapha. I apply Your truth to my body—You have already healed me.

I speak to every system of my anatomy and command it to properly align with Your plumbline of healing: cardiovascular, circulatory, digestive, endocrine, exocrine, integumentary, lymphatic, immune, muscular, nervous, pulmonary, reproductive, respiratory, skeletal, and urinary. Each system is now required to function according to the Word of God. Every organ, tissue, and cell associated with these systems functions and will continue to function perfectly, in accordance with the bruised Body and shed Blood of Jesus, the Christ. Nothing is missing and nothing is broken in my physical body.

As I meditate on and gratefully eat Your Flesh and drink Your Blood, I abide in You and You in me. I remember and honor Your selfless sacrifice by observing communion.

Triumphantly, I claim, receive, and apply the blessing of physical healing, health, and wholeness in my life because that is what You paid for. May You receive the reward of Your suffering, my King. With thanks, joy, and faith, I appropriate Your disfigured Body and healing Blood. I love You. Thank You, Jesus, for **Our Holy Covenant.**

ADONAI RAPHA RESPONDS

As I prayed in Gethsemane, My place of prayer, the agony was so great and the sorrow overwhelmed Me to the point of death, causing Me to fall to the ground. The pressure was so intense that the capillaries in My face and eyes burst, and My pores began to ooze blood. I suffered great grief, anguish, dread, and turmoil alone. My disciples were not able to watch and pray for one hour. After falling face down, in My sincere humanness and desperation, I asked the Father if it were possible for Him to take the cup away from Me, yet not what I will, but what He willed.

After I was arrested, Pilate ordered that I be scourged with a whip made of leather, embedded with metal, nails, and bone shards. The Roman soldiers were trained to bring a person to the point of death but not kill them. The violent abuse I endured exposed My bones, muscles, and organs. The beating ripped masses of Flesh off My bones and tore into My muscle. The vicious chastisement I suffered left My Body so disfigured that My form was beyond human likeness.

I was brutally beaten and bruised.

I bled internally and externally. I was despised and rejected—a Man of deep sorrows, intimately acquainted with suffering. The crowds were disgusted by Me, and even some of My friends turned their backs on Me.

After the scourging, I was subjected to further physical and psychological torment where they mockingly dressed Me in a purple robe and twisted a dense branch with thorns as sharp as nails, fashioning it into a crown and placing it on My head. They used a staff and struck Me again and again, driving the thorns deeper into My head, puncturing Me all over My scalp. More Blood profusely poured down My face, neck, shoulders, and back, flowing into My already lacerated, bleeding wounds and tortured Body. They beat Me with their fists and tore out portions of My beard, while spitting on Me.

They led Me out of the city and though My Body was weak from the torture, I carried the heavy beam across My shoulders to the place called Golgotha. Stripped of My clothes and lying on My back with My shoulders on the crossbeam, the Roman executioners drove large iron spikes through My wrists and feet, severing skin, nerves, and tendons, causing excruciating pain. As they lifted the cross upward, although none of My bones were broken, My joints were dislocated. Those present read the inscription above My head: Jesus of Nazareth, King of the Jews.

I hung there for six hours, struggling to breathe, enduring intense suffering. I refused their wine mixed with myrrh to ease the pain.

For three hours, darkness covered the earth. I shouted out to My Father, "My God, My God, why have You forsaken Me?"

When I knew that I had fulfilled the Messianic prophecies and sacrifice, again, I cried out with a loud agonized voice, "Tetelestai!" and sovereignly dismissed My Spirit from My Body in submission to My Father's plan. The veil of the temple was torn from top to bottom, and the earth shook.

I was buried in a borrowed tomb, and three days later, I rose from the dead, defeating death, Hell, and the grave.

I AM ALIVE!

Do you understand what I have done for you?

I bore your weaknesses and grief. I willingly carried your sorrows and endured the torment of your sufferings. Though they viewed Me as a criminal worthy of punishment, I never sinned. I was pierced for your rebellious deeds and transgressions. I was crushed for your iniquities and sin. I was beaten so you could be completely whole, experiencing peace, prosperity, and well-being. I was whipped so you could be healed. I broke every curse for you. There is no accident, injury, infirmity, disease, or sickness I cannot heal. I am greater than all of these; they must bow down to Me.

My Name is the only Name that death, hell, and the grave bow down to.

Stand in the healing I have already provided for you. When I cried out, "Tetelestai! It is finished!" do you understand that I finished paying for everything you would ever need? I have paid your debt in full. Healing belongs to you. You do not have to attain it.

Healing is part of My atonement for you, just like salvation. Now, receive it.

Never doubt what My will is. My Word is clear. Healing is My perfect will for My children. Healing is your birthright.

When you diligently listen and pay attention to My voice, follow My commandments, and obey My precepts, then diseases and sickness cannot plague you. The enemy loses his power when You embrace My sacrifice. I call Myself Adonai Rapha. I am the Lord Who Heals.

I was your Healer. I am your Healer. I will always be your Healer.

Just as I spoke the word to the Roman officer regarding his son, so I also speak the same encouragement to you! "Go! All that you have believed for will be done for you!"

My Body was broken so that yours could be completely whole, healthy, and healed. I am more than enough for you. I was willing to endure it all because I love you. To me, beloved, you are worthy of My sacrifice. There is nothing I would not do for you.

In your distress you cried out to Me, and I saved you from all your distresses. I sent My Word and healed you, and rescued you from your destruction.

Now, speak. Do not stop. Claim your healing, yes, but do not stop there. Do what I told you. You do not have to beg for your healing. It is already yours. Instead, command your healing to manifest in your body! Speak to that mountain. Speak to your body. Tell your body what My Word says. Tell your body what I did. Speak to that sickness, that infirmity, that disease, that mountain, and tell it what it can do and where it can go.

Now, advance forward and enforce My triumph, which My Body and Blood purchased for you. My sacrifice on the cross secured everything you need.

I am Adonai Rapha, the Lord Who Heals. This is your inheritance from Me. I am your Healer. You are healed! This is My promise to you sealed by **Our Holy Covenant.**

Scripture references—Psalm 103, Peter 2, 1 Corinthians 6, Exodus 15, Galatians 3, Romans 8, Psalm 139, Psalm 22, Mark 15, Mark 16, Matthew 26, John 6, Matthew 8, Mark 5

Visit www.amandahill.org or scan the QR code below. Partake of the elements and then listen to the worship song that coincides with Day #9.

TASTE AND SEE

Have you been struggling with physical sickness? Speak to that part of your body and believe in faith that Jesus has already healed you. Now, take time throughout the next week, say out loud that you receive His healing touch, and thank Him in advance.

Is there someone you know that needs healing in their body? Part of the great commission and its proceeding promise in Mark 16 is laying hands on the sick, and they will get well. Consider gathering a few believers and go pray for the sick person(s).

Decree Against Terminal Diagnosis

I repent of my sins and release forgiveness to anyone who has trespassed against me. Holy Spirit, wash my heart of all unforgiveness, bitterness, and resentment. In Your Name, I close any open doors to the enemy and remove his legal rights to my body and soul.

Jesus, because of You, I am an overcomer. I overcome this terminal report by the Blood of the Lamb and the word of my testimony. Just like David did before he faced Goliath, I prophesy how my battle with this disease will end: I will triumph over the enemy of disease because Jesus's pierced Body declares that He has already healed me! I renounce this negative report and cancel its effect on my mind and body. I announce my alignment and agreement with the report of the Lord, who has already healed me. Adonai Rapha is my Healer.

No disease or sickness that is formed against me will succeed. I refute and condemn every hex, vex, whammy, incantation, potion, curse, spell, magic, enchantment, bewitchment, sorcery, and jinx spoken against me. This triumph is my inheritance because I belong to King Jesus! This is my vindication!

By the authority of Jesus, I speak to the spirit of premature death, Hell, and the grave, and cancel your assignment. I command you to bow to the Name of Jesus. Therefore, sickness, disease, and infirmity have no power over, on, or in me.

At Calvary, your defeat was finalized.

Jesus, You instructed me to speak to mountains and not doubt, and it will be done. So, I speak to tumors, rebellious cells, malignant growths, cysts, adhesions, mutations, and obstructions that may be thriving in my body and command them to cease growing and dissolve now in Jesus's Name.

I forbid any malfunction in my organs. My brain, heart, lungs, liver, gallbladder, kidneys, spleen, pancreas, thyroid, stomach, intestines, skin, and bladder are healed!

The abundant life of Christ flows through my body, cleansing and healing every gland, tissue, muscle, lymph node, joint, tendon, bone, and cell. Jesus, Your Blood courses through my veins, capillaries, arteries, and blood vessels, purifying my blood. I am healed from the top of my head to the soles of my feet.

I believe the report of the Lord that declares, "TETELESTAI! I AM HEALED!"

Decree for Women During the Change of Life

Nothing is too hard for You, Adonai Rapha! There is no condition, symptom, or hormonal shift that can stand against Your powerful Name. When You allowed Your Body to be pierced and Your Blood to be spilled, You broke the curse associated with sin that was pronounced in the Garden of Eden. Jesus, You paid the full ransom price to set me free. Your perfect sacrifice on the cross redeemed me from the effects of any and all curses.

I lay hold of the power of your curse-breaking Body and Blood on behalf of the changes occurring in my hormones.

I speak to my body and command it to align with the law of the Spirit of life in Christ Jesus. I break agreement with and am free from the law of sin and death. Therefore, any tormenting symptoms associated with perimenopause, premenopause, menopause, and postmenopause may not touch me. I sever the curse and forbid hot flashes, night sweats, urinary issues, mood swings, depression, digestive issues, anxiety, dry eyes, insomnia, arthritis, headaches, fatigue, suicidal thoughts, weight gain, acne, hair loss, vaginal dryness, brain fog, irritability, fatty liver disease, inflammation, mental health disorders, frozen shoulder, vertigo, nausea, heartburn, decreased libido, heart palpitations, joint and muscle pain, allergies, osteoporosis, and any other symptom associated with this change.

These issues are a result of the curse, which I am not under. I am under and have been washed in the Blood of Jesus.

Adonai, thank You for the close circle of family and friends who are supportive, understanding, and patient during this progression. The enemy may not wreak havoc through misunderstandings or hurt feelings. In Your Name, I forbid the spirit of strife or Leviathan from causing relational drama.

Thank You for the medical professionals who work hard. However, they only practice medicine. You are the great Physician, Adonai Rapha, the Lord Who Heals. I cancel the spirit of dread and do not agree with what modern medicine decides regarding this process in my body, which is Your temple. Instead, I speak to my body and declare that this transition will not be harsh, and it will not last years. I command my body to shift gently, kindly, swiftly and without difficulty.

Body, you will produce the correct amounts of estrogen, progesterone, and testosterone according to the timeline that Adonai Rapha has set for me. Father, You created my body and desire to see me walk in wholeness. Therefore, I will eat foods that help, not hurt Your temple. Teach me to listen to Your Spirit so that I will triumph in this new phase of my life. Thank You that **Our Holy Covenant** has secured my health, healing, and wholeness.

DAY 10

PLUNDER THE ENEMY

EXODUS 3:22, EXODUS 12:33-35

EL G'MULOT, The God of Recompense

I SPEAK

Thank You, Jesus, for Your sacrifice. I remember and meditate on the price You paid for me. The New Covenant, purchased by Your Body and Blood, serves as my weapon for warring triumphantly. In humility, I confess my sins and ask for Your forgiveness. In Your mercy, cleanse my heart, mind, words, behavior, and anything that contradicts Your character and Holy Spirit. Acquit me of my unconscious, unintended faults. According to the greatness of Your compassion, blot out my transgressions. Wash me thoroughly from my wickedness, guilt, and iniquity.

I receive Your promise of plundering the enemy and his kingdom through Your Body and Blood!

Everything that has been stolen must be repaid with interest! The enemy is a thief who has been caught, and now El G'Mulot, the God of Recompense, and I demand that the thief repay me seven times what he has stolen. I decree that the enemy must surrender all the property and possessions of his kingdom to repay his debt to me. I command that where Satan has stolen, killed, and destroyed in my life, his deeds are now exposed by the powerful authority of the Body and Blood of Jesus, the Messiah. Thank You, Jesus, for Your extraordinary sacrifice, which empowers me with the right to demand that the enemy return what he has robbed from me. I am so thankful that You came so that I might enjoy life and have it in abundance—full and overflowing. Holy Spirit, reveal to me the areas where the enemy has picked my pocket and stolen from me, whether it be small or great.

I am officially and decisively reclaiming every aspect of my life: my health, my children, my finances, my marriage, my mental well-being, my authority, my home, my faith, my rest, my relationships, my purpose, my hope, my insights, my dreams, my business, my joy, my territory, my strength, my peace, my ministry, my time, my inheritance, my vision, and any other areas where I have faced loss. I am determined to seize and recover all that is rightfully mine!

My threshing floors will overflow with bountiful harvests, and my vats shall overflow with vibrant new wine and rich fresh oil. Thank You, Father, for the revelation that Your Body and Blood serve as my mighty weapons, mandating restitution from the clutches of the kingdom of darkness. I welcome Your supernatural intervention to restore and rejuvenate what has been devastated in my life.

I have entered into my era of divine recovery, where my physical, spiritual, relational, financial, social, and mental assets are exponentially increasing and flourishing far beyond their former state!

I am not helpless! I shake off the effects of the heavy shadows and hope deferred from the last season of loss. I appeal to Heaven! I shall plunder the enemy and use the spoils against him and his cohorts. Hell will not prevail against El G'Mulot. King Jesus prevails!

As I remember the sacrifice of Jesus, the Son of God, I claim and gratefully receive the blessing of plundering the enemy and recovering seven times the spoils for what was stolen.

Let the era of ransacking and recovering all begin!

As I meditate on and gratefully eat Your Flesh and drink Your Blood, I abide in You and You in me. I remember and honor Your selfless sacrifice by observing communion.

Triumphantly, I claim, receive, and apply the blessing of plundering the enemy's camp because that is what You paid for. May You receive the reward of Your suffering, my King. With thanks, joy, and faith, I appropriate Your wounded Body and redemptive Blood. I love You. Thank You, Jesus, for **Our Holy Covenant.**

EL G'MULOT REPLIES

It fills Me with hilarious joy to watch you boldly expose the enemy, asserting My power and overcoming him with matchless strength. My covenant paid for you to have that privilege of putting him in his rightful place, which is under your feet. I have witnessed the years of devastation that you have endured. But now, I, El G'Mulot, will make up for those years in which the outbreak of locusts devoured and ruined your harvest—the swarming locust with its chaotic flight, the creeping locust that silently destroys, the stripping locust that leaves nothing behind, and the gnawing locust that feasts on what remains.

Listen to My promise to you, My favored one. I will richly compensate you for every loss, and your fields shall flourish again.

The enemy, equipped with weapons and guards, considers his stolen treasures out of your reach, safe from your reclaiming. However, I have given you the strength and strategy to rise up to pursue, overtake, rescue, and recover all! You shall overpower him! You possess the authority to storm and possess the gates of the enemy, dismantling his oppressive, thieving tyranny in your life!

> You are a conqueror and are called to ransack his kingdom, seize the plunder, and then distribute all the spoils of victory.

I proclaim that all who seek to devour you will find themselves devoured; every adversary you face will be captured and brought low into captivity.

Those who plunder your treasures will themselves be stripped of their wealth, and all who hunt you down will become prey in the hands of My justice.

Now, advance forward and enforce My triumph, which My Body and Blood purchased for you. My sacrifice on the cross secured everything you need.

I am El G'Mulot, the God of Recompense Who imparts you with everything you need to plunder the enemy's camp! This is your inheritance from Me. You will take back everything that was stolen from you! This is My promise to you sealed by **Our Holy Covenant.**

Scripture references—Proverbs 6, Joel 2, Malachi 3, Isaiah 49, Jeremiah 30, Luke 11, Deuteronomy 20:14, Exodus 15:9, Matthew 11, 2 Kings 7, Genesis 22, John 6

Visit www.amandahill.org or scan the QR code below. Partake of the elements and then listen to today's worship song that coincides with Day #10.

TASTE AND SEE

From the list above, choose an area in your life where the enemy has robbed from you and write it below. If there is something specific that the enemy took from you that is not mentioned, write it down.

Now, in your own words, write and then speak aloud your decree of reclaiming what has been stolen from you.

DAY 11

VISION AND THE WORD OF THE LORD

GENESIS 14:17–15:7, LUKE 24:13–35

ADONAI CHAZON, Lord of Vision

I OPEN

Thank You, Jesus, for Your sacrifice. I remember and meditate on the price You paid for me. The New Covenant, purchased by Your Body and Blood, serves as my weapon for warring triumphantly. In humility, I confess my sins and ask for Your forgiveness. In Your mercy, cleanse my heart, mind, words, behavior, and anything that contradicts Your character and Holy Spirit. Acquit me of my unconscious, unintended faults. According to the greatness of Your compassion, blot out my transgressions. Wash me thoroughly from my wickedness, guilt, and iniquity.

I receive Your promise of vision and Your Word in my life through Your Body and Blood!

Just as Abraham received the bread and the wine from Melchizedek, the priest of Salem, and then the Word of the Lord came to him in a vision, so I also receive this blessing in my life. I believe that when I remember Your sacrifice, You reveal Yourself as Adonai Chazon, the Lord of Vision. Sanctify my eye and ear gates. Holy Spirit, open my eyes so I can clearly recognize You. Let my heart be filled with passion as You reveal Your plans and purposes for my life.

Your Word is true. Where there is no clear prophetic vision, no revelation of You and Your Word, it is easy for people to wander astray and perish. When I follow the revelation of Your Word, my soul is filled with joy!

I will write what You show me so those who read it will be inspired to run with endurance. Even though the vision You have revealed to me might be for a future time, it will be fulfilled and will not fail. If it seems to be delayed, I will patiently wait for it to manifest, confident that it will certainly happen because You are not a man that You should lie.

I admit that I have many plans regarding Your purpose for my life, but I understand that it is Your purpose that will stand and prevail. I commit my way to You and trust You to bring it to fruition. I commit my works to You, and my plans will succeed. Thank You for directing my steps and establishing my path.

I ask You to clarify Your vision for my life and for You to confirm it through Your Word. I will not allow the enemy to rob me of Your vision for my life. My destiny is at stake, and I will not relent.

I am determined to fulfill the purpose for which You created me.

I declare that I am vertically and horizontally aligned with Your will, timing, and the right people. Adonai Chazon, You knew and saw who You created me to be before I was even born. My days and my purpose were written in the book You authored for me. I will not leave this earth prematurely; I will accomplish all that You have written and planned for me.

As I seek Your will for my life, You place Your visions and dreams within me. Let me see what You see. Let me dream what You dream.

Dream through me. Help me fulfill the dream You have for my life.

I will be discerning about whom I share my visions and dreams with. Adonai Chazon, assist me in my pursuit of wise counsel. Impart to me creative ideas that will help bring to fruition what You have placed within me. Stir my imagination so that I may dream Your dreams!

I command my faith to increase so that I can align and agree with the vision You have given to me. I will diligently listen to, meditate on, and speak Your Word so that my faith will flourish. Your Word is living, active, and full of power. It is sharper than any two-edged sword, penetrating to the core of my being where soul and spirit, bone and marrow meet. Your Word exposes and judges true thoughts and secret motives. Let Your Word expose and judge me, Holy Spirit.

It is impossible for Your Word to return void; it must accomplish what You desire and succeed in the matters for which You sent it. I lean into and embrace the truth of Your Word; as I do this, my faith grows exponentially.

The visions and dreams You have given me are assignments; they are not my god, lord, or taskmaster. I submit to and serve You, not my assignments.

I was created to love You and fulfill
Your purposes for my life.

Thank You for planning so many things for me so long ago. I am convinced and confident that the good work You have begun in me, You will continue to perfect and complete until the day You return. May every plan and purpose for my future succeed.

Lord, You are my greatest treasure. I will not allow my vision to become greater than You. I was created to know, serve, and love You. I want to see You. I want to know You. I want to love You. You are my vision. You are my dream.

When I break the bread and partake of Your mutilated Body, You command the scales and blinders to fall off, and I can see You. Thank You for supernaturally opening my eyes and restoring my vision.

As I meditate on and gratefully eat Your Flesh and drink Your Blood, I abide in You and You in me. I remember and honor Your selfless sacrifice by observing communion.

Triumphantly, I claim, receive, and apply the blessing of vision and the Word of the Lord in my life because that is what You paid for. May You receive the reward of Your suffering, my King. With thanks, joy, and faith, I appropriate Your tortured Body and pure Blood. I love You. Thank You, Jesus, for **Our Holy Covenant.**

ADONAI CHAZON RESPONDS

I am a visionary, and you inherited My visionary nature because we are one. You are part of My vision to change the world. I designed you to see a need and be a part of the solution. My vision gives you purpose.

I am the Architect of the blueprints for your life. When others see problems or obstacles, you see possibilities and opportunities! Nothing is impossible for you when you submit to Me.

You are My greatest masterpiece. You are truly a work of art, reborn from above and spiritually transformed for good works, which I have prepared. You will walk on the path I have made ready for you.

I have empowered you with everything you need! I created you with abilities, gifts, the perfect personality, and a drive to succeed.

Realize that when you submit to Me, I place My vision and dreams for your life within you. I am the Visionary to your vision. I am the Dreamer of your dreams. Understand that I am in this process with you. I am for you.

When you call to Me, I will answer you and reveal great and mighty things, things which have been confined and hidden, which you do not know or understand and cannot distinguish. I know the plans and thoughts that I have for you. My plans are for peace and well-being, not disaster, to give you a future and a hope.

Do not lose hope! There will be giants who try to stop you from accomplishing your vision. They are your bread. So, view them as such!

Remember, that I can do superabundantly more than all you could ever ask, envision, think, dream, pray, or believe, according to My power that is at work within you.

Every heavenly opportunity will be met with demonic opposition. So, do not give up, retreat, or relent. The test of delay will come, but you will pass it with persevering patience by relying on Me.

Together, we have got this.

Now, advance forward and enforce My triumph, which My Body and Blood purchased for you. My sacrifice on the cross secured everything you need.

I am Adonai Chazon, the Lord of Vision, Who imparts My prophetic Word to you because you are Mine! This is your inheritance from Me. I give you vision and My Word. This is My promise to you sealed by **Our Holy Covenant.**

Scripture References—Proverbs 29, Habakkuk 2, Jeremiah 29, Proverbs 19, Ephesians 3, Ephesians 2, Acts 2:17, Psalm 37, Jeremiah 33, Philippians 1, Proverbs 16, Hebrews 4, Isaiah 55, Psalm 139, Numbers 23, John 6

Visit www.amandahill.org or scan the QR code below. Partake of the elements and then listen to the worship song that coincides with Day #11.

TASTE AND SEE

Do you know what your God-ordained purpose is? If yes, are you actively pursuing and fulfilling it? If not, what is holding you back?

If you answered no to the first part of question number 1, begin a dialogue with Holy Spirit. Ask Him to show you His plan for your life. During the upcoming communion time, intentionally welcome His vision to unfold and His Voice to speak. Record all He shows you.

DAY 12

PROVISION

EXODUS 16:1–21, JOSHUA 5:10–12, 2 CHRONICLES 31:5–11

ADONAI JIREH, The Lord Who Provides

I BEGIN

Thank You, Jesus, for Your sacrifice. I remember and meditate on the price You paid for me. The New Covenant, purchased by Your Body and Blood, serves as my weapon for warring triumphantly. In humility, I confess my sins and ask for Your forgiveness. In Your mercy, cleanse my heart, mind, words, behavior, and anything that contradicts Your character and Holy Spirit. Acquit me of my unconscious, unintended faults. According to the greatness of Your compassion, blot out my transgressions. Wash me thoroughly from my wickedness, guilt, and iniquity.

I receive Your promise of providing all the provision I need in my life through Your Body and Blood!

You are the God of abundance! I am anointed to prosper. I seek Your Kingdom and the righteous way of doing things, and You will provide everything I need and more.

You know exactly what I need before I even ask because You are a good Father, and it is Your good pleasure to give me the Kingdom. Blessing me brings You joy!

Giving flows from my heart, not from a religious duty or obligation. It springs up freely from the joy of giving because I know You love hilarious generosity. I give generously, and generous gifts will be poured back into my lap, measured out in abundance, pressed down, shaken together, and running over with no space left for more! Abundant gifts will pour upon me with such an overflowing measure that it will run over the top. The measure that I pour out will be the measure returned to me. Therefore, I am an extreme giver!

Thank You that my heavenly account
is accumulating with every gift I sow.

You, Adonai Jireh, are the Lord Who Provides all my needs according to Your riches in Glory. You make all grace abound toward me so that I always have more than enough for all You have placed within my heart.

My harvest is protected because I choose to give! In faith, I bring my tithes and offerings into Your storehouse, and as a result, You open the windows of Heaven and pour out such blessings on me that there is not enough room to contain them. Because I am a joyful giver, You rebuke the devourer for my sake. Thank You! I am a servant of Yours, Adonai Jireh.

> I do not serve mammon, money, possessions, fame, status, or anything that tries to take Your place, King Jesus.

Dagon, the false god of abundance, is dethroned in my life. I declare that Dagon is beheaded and his hands are amputated, in Jesus's Name. I decree that his false authority and demonic supply lines are severed now. I cut off the head of the python spirit that has tried to squeeze breath, life, dreams, ideas, creativity, opportunities, provision, abundance, and resources from me. The slithering, manipulating days of this spirit are over. I am not Leviathan's prey. On the contrary, the Lord has crushed this serpent and given him to me as my food. I have divine victory. In Jesus's Name, I attack lack and every demon that attempts to block, delay, or deny my provision. I serve notice to the kingdom of darkness—Jesus defeated you, and so have I.

I repent, Jesus. Please forgive me for the moments when I acted out of selfishness, disobedience, greed, recklessness, or laziness, letting the gifts You entrusted to me slip through my fingers. Purify my heart, Lord. Today, I make a heartfelt commitment to honor and nurture all You have provided. I will be a good steward of what You have entrusted to me. I repent for allowing generational curses of poverty, debt, failure, and lack to linger and remain in my bloodline. I owe no man anything but to love him. I apply the powerful Blood of Jesus to cleanse this iniquity and generational mindset from my family line. I renounce and revoke the agreement the enemy has had on me, my children, my children's children, and beyond. I now loose the blessing, provision, wealth, and abundance of King Jesus in my life and in the lives of my family members.

Poverty ends with me, and abundant provision begins with me.

Adonai Jireh, send me dreams and visions of how to create and birth witty inventions, receive breakthrough ideas, and state-of-the-art innovation that will bring generational prosperity to my family!

You have given me the keys to the Kingdom of Heaven. Whatever I bind and forbid on Earth shall have already been bound and forbidden in Heaven. Whatever I loose and permit on Earth has already been loosed and permitted in Heaven. I come into alignment with Heaven and Heaven's provision. Poverty is bound, and provision is loosed in my life.

I yield my resources and finances to the economy of Heaven. I am not limited or bound by this world's economy. I submit my finances, prosperity, abundance, and provision to Your rule, Your Kingdom, and Your ways.

Your Presence is welcome and abides in my home.

Therefore, I am under Your blessing just like Obed-Edom. Everything I possess is supernaturally blessed. I diligently listen to and obey Your Voice, ensuring I am careful to do all You command. Therefore, you set me high above all the nations of the earth. Blessings come upon me and overtake me because I pay attention to Your Voice. I am blessed in the city and blessed in the field. My children are blessed, and my produce, animals, herds, and flocks are blessed. My baskets and kneading bowls are blessed as well. I am blessed coming in and blessed going out. You cause the enemies who rise up against me to be defeated before me; they may come at me one way, but they will flee before me in seven ways.

Adonai Jireh, You command the blessing upon me in my storehouses and in all that I undertake. You grant me great prosperity. You open for me Your good treasure house, the heavens, to give rain on my land in its season and bless all the work of my hands. I will lend to many nations, but I will borrow from none. You make me the head and not the tail. I am only above and not beneath. I have more coming in than I have going out.

As I remember You, You give me the power, the dreams, and the creativity to create wealth, confirming **Your Holy Covenant** with me.

I decree that I will leave an inheritance to my children and my children's children.

I look to You as my Provider. My job, business, and boss are not my providers—You are! They are just an avenue You use to bless me.

I repent of a poverty mentality. I surrender any patterns of lack, famine or deficiency in my thought life. Please rewire those pathways in my brain with Your truth.

You, Oh, Lord, are the Breaker, and You go before me, opening the way, liberating me.

I receive Your gift of Holy Spirit in my life. I now access wisdom, understanding, knowledge, revelation, insight, ideas, clarity, opportunities, relationships, and all the skills needed to create everything You have called me to.

I am a problem solver, an obstacle remover, and a prophetic strategist. I understand the times and the seasons and what should and should not be done.

The wealth of the wicked has been stored up and is now being transferred to me because I stand in Your righteousness, Jesus. I am in the right place at the right time to receive this blessing. Goodness and mercy chase me down and overtake me. I am contagiously, abundantly, supernaturally blessed.

Imprint my heart with Your purposes.

Speak, Lord, I am listening.

I command increase and blessings to manifest in my life. I speak death to drought, lack, and debt in my life. I speak life, abundance, and enlargement to my finances and resources.

As I meditate on and gratefully eat Your Flesh and drink Your Blood, I abide in You and You in me. I remember and honor Your selfless sacrifice by observing communion.

Triumphantly, I claim, receive, and apply the blessing of abundant provision by my Amazing Provider in my life because that is what You paid for. May You receive the reward of Your suffering, my King. With thanks, joy, and faith, I appropriate Your ransomed Body and sinless Blood. I love You. Thank You, Jesus, for **Our Holy Covenant.**

ADONAI JIREH RESPONDS

My covenant purchased and provided abundant provision, eradicating poverty from your life. I promise to fully satisfy your every need according to My glorious riches. Did I not demonstrate My love for you? I am My Father's greatest treasure, and He gave Me for you—My life for yours, and you are worth it.

Everything I possess belongs to you!

The nails driven through My hands, slicing joints and ligaments, redeemed your ability to succeed, prosper, and receive divine inheritance.

You are an overcomer because I conquered death, Hell, and the grave. Therefore, nothing can overcome and defeat you. Remember to submit yourself to Me, resist the enemy and he must flee from you.

I have chosen and anointed you to be a disruptor of the enemy's strategies on how he will fund his dark kingdom and agenda. You will interrupt, unsettle, and dismantle systems, companies, businesses, processes, events, and structures that he has built, as they do not align with My purpose. They do not belong to Me, but you do. So, I will put you in situations that will make people wonder how you achieved such rapid advancement. You are my instrument who will uproot, tear down, destroy, and overthrow. Stay in My flow and My timing, and I will advance you supernaturally.

I want you to embrace and thrive in the provision, authority, favor, and destiny that I have made available to you through the finished work of the cross.

I rebuke the devourers that have been sent against you.

You are not a beggar. You are not an orphan. I no longer call you "servant," but I have called you My friend because I have confided in you, revealing to you all that I have heard from Our Father.

I will make you resilient against economic challenges. Do not submit your finances to the world's economy. It will certainly falter. However, My Kingdom economy will never collapse. Embrace and submit to My ways, in My time, and in My economy. You are recession and depression proof as you surrender your life to e. What affects others will not affect you, for I protect you.

I have given you everything you need because you have the keys to the Kingdom, which will unlock resources, provision, and abundance.

I provided manna and meat for My people. I also brought forth fresh, clean, flowing water from a rock. What I did for them, I am more than able to do the same for you. I am the God who gives you land you did not labor for, with excellent and splendid cities you did not build, houses full of good things you did not furnish, wells you did not dig, and vineyards you did not plant. I will cause deeds, titles, and large lump sums of money to be given to you. I have called you to take dominion and be the master over the resources I have placed in your hands.

You were not created to survive, but to thrive. I am Adonai Jireh, your Provider.

Everything belongs to Me. All the animals of the forest are Mine, and I own the cattle on a thousand hills. I know every bird of the mountains, and everything that moves in the field is Mine. There is nothing that I have that does not belong to you.

Now, advance forward and enforce My triumph, which My Body and Blood purchased for you. My sacrifice on the cross secured everything you need.

I am Adonai Jireh, the Lord Who Provides, overwhelming you with abundant provision! This is your inheritance from Me. I am your Provider. I will provide for you. This is My promise to you sealed by **Our Holy Covenant.**

Scripture references—Romans 8, Matthew 6, Luke 16, Proverbs 13, Exodus 31, Deuteronomy 8, Micah 2, Luke 6, 2 Corinthians 9, Philippians 4, Deuteronomy 6, Joshua 24, Deuteronomy 28, Romans 13, Proverbs 24, 2 Chronicles 20, Genesis 50, Zechariah 4, James 4, Psalm 74, John 15, Matthew 20

Visit www.amandahill.org or scan the QR code below. Partake of the elements and then listen to the worship song that coincides with Day #12.

TASTE AND SEE

This is a time when the Lord is raising up Kingdom entrepreneurs and business owners. Have you ever had a promising idea, witty invention, or creative solution you knew you should pursue, but have not done so yet? If so, what is it and why have you not moved forward?

Are you currently struggling with doubt regarding how Adonai Jireh desires to bless, prosper, and provide for you? Take a few moments to repent and submit your doubt and unbelief to Him. Ask Him to show you how He wants to prosper you.

Decree for Kingdom Entrepreneurs and Business Owners

I dedicate my businesses, companies, and enterprises to You, Adonai Jireh. I withhold nothing from You. I will conduct my business dealings with fairness, generosity, honor, and honesty.

I will be on the cutting edge of technology to expand and increase what You have entrusted me to steward. My businesses will fulfill their purpose in advancing and funding Kingdom initiatives and exploits!

I will not despise the day of small beginnings. I believe in the dreams and visions You gave me to triumph in my business. We will give generously!

I will enjoy what You have called me to do and prioritize wisely.

> The success of my endeavors is not by might, nor by power, but by the Spirit of the living God!

I release the wind and fire of God against the enemies that would attempt to hinder and stop my advancement.

Thank You for turning around the evil and harm that the enemy intended against my business and making it work for my good. I trust You!

I believe in and trust in You, Lord. Therefore, I am established and secure. I believe in, listen to, and trust in Your prophets, and I will succeed.

I will operate with integrity, for a spirit of excellence is present in all I do.

Where wicked businesses have robbed and gained wealth, let that wealth be transferred to businesses that operate righteously. My business will be a light for the gospel, and we will not be ashamed to share our faith in You, Jesus!

I am a wise builder. My enterprises, companies, and businesses are established, endure, and excel through apostolic intelligence, wise counsel, and prophetic insight. I am a skilled leader. My employees embody wisdom, honor, and a strong work ethic.

I break the spirits of sabotage, failure, distractions, rejection, seduction, dishonor, and small-mindedness from myself and my employees. I command all word curses and false prophetic words to fall to the ground, sterile and ineffective.

I am in alignment with Your timing and plans, Adonai Jireh. I thank You that new deals and contracts are supernaturally falling into my lap, and I forbid any snares and traps from baiting me. Real estate deals will be in my favor. My liabilities are decreasing, and my assets are increasing. I am moving from the red to the black.

Thank you, Adonai Jireh, for blessing the work of my hands. It all belongs to You.

DAY 13

CONSECRATION

EXODUS 19:1-11, JOHN 13:5-10

EL KADOSH, Holy God

EL KADOSH INITIATES

Because you have chosen to obey My voice and keep My covenant, you are My special treasure, called for My sacred purpose. I have chosen you. You are part of My royal priesthood, a consecrated, holy nation, and a special people for My possession. You are anointed to proclaim My excellent and perfect deeds.

If anyone is in Me, joined to Me by faith, he is a new creature, reborn and renewed by My Spirit. Everything old has passed away.

Behold, new things have come because
spiritual awakening brings new life!

Not everyone who calls Me "Lord" will enter the Kingdom of Heaven, but only the ones who do the will of My Father. Even if they prophesy, drive out demons, and work miracles in My Name, I will declare on the Day of Judgment that I never knew them. The ones who abide in My Word and obey My teachings are My disciples. They are those who know Me intimately and are saved.

My will for you is that you be sanctified, consecrated, separated, and set apart from sin. That you know how to control your body in holiness and honor, being available for My purposes. I have not called you to impurity, but to holiness, set apart by behavior that pleases Me, whether in public or private. I want you to imitate Me, as beloved children imitate their father.

I have provided everything you need for a life of holiness, consecration, and godliness through My divine power and the knowledge of My Son, Jesus. You are called to be in the world, not of it. Do not allow the world to corrupt you. Receive My Spirit to help you accomplish having clean hands and a pure heart.

Now, advance forward and enforce My triumph, which My Body and Blood purchased for you. My sacrifice on the cross secured everything you need.

I am El Kadosh, the Holy God Who has called you to be like Me, holy. This is your inheritance from Me. I will make you holy. You are holy. This is My promise to you sealed by **Our Holy Covenant.**

I ANSWER

Thank You, Jesus, for Your sacrifice. I remember and meditate on the price You paid for me. The New Covenant, purchased by Your Body and Blood, serves as my weapon for warring triumphantly. In humility, I confess my sins and ask for Your forgiveness. In Your mercy, cleanse my heart, mind, words, behavior, and anything that contradicts Your character and Holy Spirit. Acquit me of my unconscious, unintended faults. According to the greatness of Your compassion, blot out my transgressions. Wash me thoroughly from my wickedness, guilt, and iniquity.

I receive Your promise of consecration in my life through Your Body and Blood!

I am called to freedom. I will not allow my freedom to become an opportunity for sin to flourish. I desire to ascend to Your mountain, Lord! Clean my hands and purify my heart! I will not lift up my soul to what is false, nor swear oaths deceitfully.

Today, I make a choice to follow Your righteous example. I vow to:

- walk continually in love;
- practice compassion;
- unselfishly seek the best for others;
- have nothing to do with sexual immorality, moral impurity, or offensive behavior;
- allow no filthiness, silly talk, or vulgar joking to come out of my mouth;

- refrain from empty, worldly arguments;
- not participate in worthless and unproductive deeds of darkness, but instead expose them; and
- never use my words to lie, gossip, slander, or flatter.

I will continuously walk in and with Your Presence. I command my flesh to submit to my spirit, which is guided and governed by Your Holy Spirit. My spirit opposes my sinful nature. Although my flesh and spirit are in direct conflict with each other, Your Spirit within me prevails in this struggle every single time!

I refuse the practices of the sinful nature: sexual immorality, impurity, sensuality, lack of self-control, idolatry, sorcery, hostility, strife, jealousy, fits of anger, disputes, dissensions, factions, envy, drunkenness, riotous behavior, and other things like these.

I produce the fruit of Your Spirit:
love, joy, peace, patience, kindness,
goodness, faithfulness, gentleness, and self-control.

Your Word promises that the pure in heart get to see You. That is the cry of my heart, seeing and knowing You! Wash me in Your love until I am pure in heart.

I know that You delight in setting Your truth deep within my spirit. So come into the hidden places of my heart and teach me wisdom.

Satisfy me with Your sweetness, and my song of joy will return. The places You have crushed within me will rejoice in Your healing touch.

Continue creating in me a clean heart. Fill me with pure thoughts and holy desires, ready to please You.

Let my passion for life be renewed, and I will find joy in every breakthrough You bring me. Hold me close with a willing spirit that obeys Your every command. Then I can show others who feel guilty how loving and merciful You are. They will find their way home to You, knowing you will forgive them.

El Kadosh, unlock my heart and lips, and I will overflow with joyous praise! The source of Your pleasure does not come from my performance or the sacrifices I might offer you. Your true pleasure is found in the sacrifice of my broken heart before You. You will not despise my humility as I bow down at Your feet.

I will be like the Holy One who called me. In all my conduct, I will be set apart from the world by my godly character and moral courage.

As I meditate on and gratefully eat Your Flesh and drink Your Blood, I abide in You and You in me. I remember and honor Your selfless sacrifice by observing communion.

Triumphantly, I claim, receive, and apply the blessing of consecration in my life because that is what You paid for. May You receive the reward of Your suffering, my King. With thanks, joy, and faith, I appropriate Your beaten Body and atoning Blood. I love You. Thank You, Jesus, for **Our Holy Covenant.**

Scripture references—1 Peter 2, Exodus 19, Psalm 51, 2 Corinthians 5, Ephesians 5, Galatians 5, Ephesians 4, Psalm 24, 1 Peter 1, 1 Thessalonians 4, Matthew 5, Matthew 7, John 6, 2 Peter 1, John 17

Visit www.amandahill.org or scan the QR code below. Partake of the elements and then listen to the worship song that coincides with Day #13.

TASTE AND SEE

Do you struggle with any particular sin? If yes, have you asked Holy Spirit to help you overcome it? Have you been vulnerable with others, asking them to hold you accountable?

Fasting crucifies our fleshly desires. If possible, take twenty-four hours to fast and ask Holy Spirit to create a pure, clean, renewed heart in you.

DAY 14

PROPHETIC WAR STRATEGIES

EXODUS 17:8–16, JOSHUA 6, NUMBERS 10:9

ADONAI GIBBOR MILCHAMAH,
The Lord Mighty in Battle

I SPEAK

Thank You, Jesus, for Your sacrifice. I remember and meditate on the price You paid for me. The New Covenant, purchased by Your Body and Blood, serves as my weapon for warring triumphantly. In humility, I confess my sins and ask for Your forgiveness. In Your mercy, cleanse my heart, mind, words, behavior, and anything that contradicts Your character and Holy Spirit. Acquit me of my unconscious, unintended faults. According to the greatness of Your compassion, blot out my transgressions. Wash me thoroughly from my wickedness, guilt, and iniquity.

I receive Your promise of prophetic war strategies in my life through Your Body and Blood!

You are Adonai Gibbor Milchamah, the Lord Mighty in Battle, and You have designed every successful battle plan because You are the Master Strategist! I turn my ear to hear what Your Spirit is speaking, and I tune my ear to the frequency of Your sound. I focus on how, when, and where You are moving. You are the Captain of Heaven's armies and lead the line of attack.

Teach me Your ways and guide me along steady paths because of my enemies who are lurking. I trust that You will not abandon me to the desires of my adversaries. I would have lost hope if I had not believed that I would witness Your goodness, Oh Merciful King.

Sometimes, I do not fully understand Your methods, but I trust in Your sovereignty because You have never lost a battle, and You never will. In the midst of the fight, I will not be afraid, for those who are with me are more numerous than those who are with the other side.

If You, Mighty Lord, are for me, who could ever stand against me and be successful?

I welcome and will be obedient to Your blueprint and will stay in rhythm with Your tempo because this is what I need to effectively engage in this battle and emerge triumphant. I will not rush ahead of Your timing, nor will I lag behind. I will stay in step with You, for You lead the battle charge and set the pace. I am led by Your Spirit, not my mind, will, or emotions.

I choose to keep my heart pure. The enemy has no hold on me because nothing within me aligns with him. I will not be lured by offense, as it blinds and deafens me to Your Voice. Therefore, I choose forgiveness and love, for love is a powerful, prophetic war strategy.

I will do good to those who hate me. I will bless and show kindness to those who curse me, and I will pray for those who mistreat me. I will turn the other cheek and ignore insults. I refuse to retaliate. Instead, I will treat others the way I want to be treated. I will never return evil for evil or insult for insult; instead, I will bless others. Love is the most excellent way. Love wins wars.

Although Your prophetic war strategies might seem foolish to some, I recognize they are superior because Your ways and thoughts are higher than ours.

You guided Moses to hold up his arms, and as a result, Amalek was defeated.

You led Joshua to circle Jericho silently, then let out battle cries and blow shofars, causing the impenetrable walls to fall.

You directed Deborah to summon Barak, and the Canaanites were conquered through Jael's tent peg and hammer.

You reduced Gideon's army to three hundred men with shofars and torches, who prevailed against a vast army.

You instructed Jehoshaphat to send Judah first; they praised and gave thanks, and then You set ambushes against their enemies, so they never lifted a sword.

You ordered David to listen for the sound of marching in the tops of the balsam trees, and then he struck down the Philistines.

Just as You guided them and many others, You will also instruct me. Sharpen my prophetic insight and warrior edge to perceive Your battle plans.

I will not veer to the right or to the left, relying on my old, familiar weapons and war strategies.

I commit to teaching my children and the generations after me how to war, ensuring their faithfulness and obedience to Your ways, precepts, and commandments. They will have ears to hear and gain new prophetic war strategies for the battles that are before them.

It is not by might, nor by power, but by Your Spirit that I will advance.

My weapons are numerous and mighty: worship, prayer, the shout, the shofar, fasting, Your Word, Your Name, my testimony, and Your Blood. I set aside the battle plans from the last season and embrace new prophetic war strategies for the present and the future. While you never change, my ability and capacity to understand and communicate with You is constantly evolving and expanding. Therefore, I will stay in proper alignment, discerning the times and seasons, and what should be done so that Your Kingdom continues to increase, while the enemy retreats in defeat. I war "from" a place of triumph, not "to" a place of triumph.

As I meditate on and gratefully eat Your Flesh and drink Your Blood, I abide in You and You in me. I remember and honor Your selfless sacrifice by observing communion.

Triumphantly, I claim, receive, and apply the blessing of prophetic war strategies in my life because that is what You paid for. May You receive the reward of Your suffering, my King. With thanks, joy, and faith, I appropriate Your scourged Body and cleansing Blood. I love You. Thank You, Jesus, for **Our Holy Covenant.**

ADONAI GIBBOR MILCHAMAH RESPONDS

You always have the upper hand on the enemy. You always have the advantage because you have Me.

I am omniscient. I know everything: past, present, and future. I know the end from the beginning because I am The Alpha and The Omega. I have limited your enemy's knowledge.

I am omnipresent. I have no physical limitations or time constraints. I transcend time because I created it. I am everywhere, in all places, simultaneously. I have set restrictions on how your enemy can maneuver.

I am omnipotent. I have unlimited power and can do anything I desire. My abilities and power are absolute and without limitations. I have diminished your enemy's power.

You give the enemy more credit than he deserves. I know his next move even before he knows it. Ask Me, and I will tell you his secrets. Ask Me how to defeat him, and let me unfold My battle plan to you.

Now, advance forward and enforce My triumph, which My Body and Blood purchased for you. My sacrifice on the cross secured everything you need.

I am Adonai Gibbor Milchamah, the Lord Mighty in Battle, Who reveals prophetic war strategies to you! This is your inheritance from Me. You win. This is My promise to you sealed by **Our Holy Covenant.**

Scripture references—Proverbs 24, 2 Samuel 5, Isaiah 55, Judges 4, Joshua 6, Judges 7, 2 Chronicles 20, Zechariah 4, 2 Corinthians 10, 2 Kings 6, Luke 6, 1 Peter 3, Romans 12, Matthew 5, John 6

Visit www.amandahill.org or scan the QR code below. Partake of the elements and then listen to the worship song that coincides with Day #14.

TASTE AND SEE

Have you found yourself fighting a new enemy? Do you feel like you are losing the battle? If yes, have you asked the Lord which weapons and prophetic war strategies would lead you to victory.

Take the next twenty-four hours to specifically thank the Lord for victory in this battle.

DAY 15

WISDOM

EXODUS 18:17–22

ADONAI CHOKMAH, Lord of Wisdom

I OPEN

Thank You, Jesus, for Your sacrifice. I remember and meditate on the price You paid for me. The New Covenant, purchased by Your Body and Blood, serves as my weapon for warring triumphantly. In humility, I confess my sins and ask for Your forgiveness. In Your mercy, cleanse my heart, mind, words, behavior, and anything that contradicts Your character and Holy Spirit. Acquit me of my unconscious, unintended faults. According to the greatness of Your compassion, blot out my transgressions. Wash me thoroughly from my wickedness, guilt, and iniquity.

I receive Your promise of wisdom in my life
through Your Body and Blood!

I believe that I am one of Your favorites! Because I follow Your will, ways, and precepts, I delight in You. In return, You grant me wisdom, knowledge, and joy!

I desire and intentionally choose Your wisdom and divine intelligence. With wise guidance, I can engage in warfare and achieve triumphant victory, for there is safety and success in the company of many wise counselors.

Lord, grant me a good reputation through honorable behavior and divine wisdom, for it is more desirable than great riches.

I receive Your promise that Your Spirit rests upon me, the Spirit of extraordinary wisdom, the Spirit of perfect understanding, the Spirit of strategic counsel, the Spirit of authoritative might, the Spirit of revelation, and the Spirit of the reverential and obedient fear of the Lord.

I decree that I am wise and prudent because I am teachable.

I bless You, Lord, for You have counseled me. My heart instructs me in the night.

Your wisdom is a tree of life to me, and I am blessed and admired for holding it tightly.

I will treasure wisdom so that I can acquire and obtain it. I graciously welcome and embrace Your counsel, Lord. Let my heart be trained to listen when You speak. I cry out for insight and lift up my voice for understanding. I seek skillful and godly wisdom like I would search for silver and hidden treasures. I will not squander Your precious gift!

I reject the wisdom of the world because it is foolishness. Instead, You flood me with skillful and godly wisdom, as knowledge and understanding flow from Your words. You are delighted to gift me with Your wisdom.

I realize that I lack wisdom on my own. I choose to embrace sound wisdom and discretion, for they will bring life to my soul. I will walk securely along the path of life, and I will not stumble. When I lie down, I will not be afraid; my sleep will be sweet, restful and peaceful.

Because I follow Your wise guidance, I walk on straight paths, and nothing will hinder my steps, as the way is clear and open. When I run, I will not stumble.

My words bring healing because they are filled with wisdom, truth, and love. As I hold tight to wisdom, my days will be multiplied, and my years of life will increase. Thanks to Your wisdom, I am slow to anger and can easily overlook transgressions and offenses. I am open to instruction and willing to accept correction.

Holy Spirit, please grant me the riches of the Spirit of Wisdom and the Spirit of Revelation to know You through my deepening intimacy with You.

Let the light of Your truth illuminate the eyes of my imagination, flooding me with light, until I experience the complete revelation of the hope of Your calling—that is the wealth of Your glorious inheritance that You find in me!

Our Holy Covenant provides me with Your precious, supernatural wisdom. Thank You, Adonai Chokmah, for this impartation. I will not squander Your gift.

As I meditate on and gratefully eat Your Flesh and drink Your Blood, I abide in You and You in me. I remember and honor Your selfless sacrifice by observing communion.

Triumphantly, I claim, receive, and apply the blessing of divine wisdom and intelligent insight in my life because that is what You paid for. May You receive the reward of Your suffering, my King. With thanks, joy, and faith, I appropriate Your bruised Body and powerful Blood. I love You. Thank You, Jesus, for **Our Holy Covenant.**

ADONAI CHOKMAH DECLARES

I have promised that if you lack wisdom to guide a decision or circumstance, ask Me for it. I will provide you with supernatural wisdom when you ask Me in faith, without doubting.

I reserve sound wisdom for the righteous, those Who are in right relationship with Me.

Blessings pour out upon you when you find My wisdom. You gain understanding and insight as you learn from My Word, which accomplishes its purpose and does not return to Me void.

The profit from wisdom is far better than the profit of silver, and its rewards surpass even the finest gold. It is your most priceless commodity, your most precious asset. It will lead you to honor and favor, granting you grace along with a crown of beauty and glory. Wisdom is more precious than rubies; nothing you can desire compares to it. It will provide you with a long life, wealth, and honor. The ways of wisdom bring favor and peace.

By my wisdom, I founded the earth, and by my understanding, I established the heavens.

My wisdom comes from above; it is pure, spiritually undefiled, and filled with peace. It is considerate, gentle, reasonable, willing to listen, full of compassion, and produces good fruits. True wisdom is unwavering and free from self-righteous hypocrisy. It is demonstrated through good deeds done with gentleness and humility.

Now, advance forward and enforce My triumph, which My Body and Blood purchased for you. My sacrifice on the cross secured everything you need.

I am Adonai Chokmah, the Lord of Wisdom, Who imparts My supernatural wisdom to you! This is your inheritance from Me. You are wise. This is My promise to you sealed by **Our Holy Covenant.**

Scripture references—Proverbs 24, James 1, Proverbs 2, Proverbs 3, Proverbs 9, Proverbs 4, Proverbs 12, Proverbs 16, Proverbs 19, James 3, Ecclesiastes 2, Proverbs 22, Isaiah 11, Proverbs 11, Psalm 16, Ephesians 1, 1 Corinthians 3, John 6

Visit www.amandahill.org or scan the QR code below. Partake of the elements and then listen to the worship song that coincides with Day #15.

TASTE AND SEE

Have you ever found yourself in a situation where you needed another level of His divine wisdom? Did you ask Holy Spirit for an impartation of it in faith? What was the outcome of that situation?

Throughout the day, intentionally take several moments to ask and then thank Holy Spirit for a deluge of His divine wisdom and intelligent insight. Be sure to journal the outcomes.

DAY 16

BREAKS BARRENNESS

EXODUS 23:26, 1 SAMUEL 1

El Yalad, The God Who Births

This portion might not apply to you personally. However, if you know anyone who needs barrenness broken off their life, put their name(s) in this prayer and take communion on their behalf. Also, there is a specific section for women and men.

I OPEN

Thank You, Jesus, for Your sacrifice. I remember and meditate on the price You paid for me. The New Covenant, purchased by Your Body and Blood, serves as my weapon for warring triumphantly. In humility, I confess my sins and ask for Your forgiveness. In Your mercy, cleanse my heart, mind, words, behavior, and anything that contradicts Your character and Holy Spirit. Acquit me of my unconscious, unintended faults. According to the greatness of Your compassion, blot out my transgressions. Wash me thoroughly from my wickedness, guilt, and iniquity.

I receive Your promise that barrenness breaks and fruitfulness fills my life through Your Body and Blood!

You are El Yalad, the God Who Births. You created me in Your own image and likeness, forming me from the dust of the ground. Then You breathed into my nostrils the breath of life—Your breath, Your Spirit! I live, breathe, and have my being in and because of You.

You blessed me and granted me complete authority, commanding me to be fruitful, multiply, and fill the earth. I am devoted to following and obeying your commandments. Lord, in turn, You keep Your covenant of steadfast lovingkindness with me.

Lord, if there are generational sins that are delaying or denying my ability to procreate, expose them now by the Blood of Your Son. I repent for the known and unknown sins of the generations who have gone before me. Father, apply the Blood of Jesus to the transgressions and iniquities of my ancestors. I repent on their behalf. Any of their or my sins that opened the door to inflict barrenness, sterility or infertility, wash and forgive them and me, Lord. I revoke and renounce the enemy's legal rights. I declare that all generational curses affecting my reproductive health be reversed by the sinless shed Blood of the Passover Lamb, transforming those generational curses into generational blessings!

Specific for Women

You created me as female and gave me the command to be fruitful and to multiply and fill the earth. I decree that I am destined to be a mother. You performed miracles for Sarah, Hannah, Rebekah, Rachel, Samson's mother, the Shunammite woman, and Elizabeth. At one time, they were all barren, childless, their wombs closed. However, You are El Yalad, the God Who Births; therefore, my womb is also able to birth. You created me in Your image.

> Therefore, it is my inheritance
> to be abundant with children.

Just as Hannah left the Passover table at Shiloh, went to the temple and prayed, and You granted her petition by opening her womb to conceive Samuel; so also, when I remember Your covenant by observing communion, You hear my cry and open my womb and barrenness breaks.

I ask You to completely heal in me what is lacking, cursed, or wounded. I ask for a miracle in my reproductive systems, El Yalad. Infertility breaks off my life in Jesus's Name. I rebuke genetic disorders, prolapsed uterus, endometriosis, sexually transmitted diseases, uterine fibroids, polycystic ovary syndrome, ovarian cysts, ovarian cancer, sexual dysfunction, tumors, abnormal menstrual cycles, uterine polyps, adhesions, scar tissue, problems with ovulation, and any other factor that would contribute to infertility. I speak to my womb, uterus, eggs, fallopian tubes, cervix, and ovaries and command them to be healthy, whole, and healed.

You bless my womb to be fruitful. I am fertile. I am not barren, childless, or infertile. I will not suffer miscarriages or stillbirths. My womb does not work against fertility in Jesus's Name. I decree that I will experience Heaven's generous reward, as children will fill my house. My children will arise and call me blessed.

Specific for Men

You created me as male and gave me the command to be fruitful and to multiply and fill the earth. I decree that I am destined to be a father. You performed miracles for Abraham, Isaac, Jacob, Elkanah, Samson's father, and Zechariah. At one time, none of them had children. However, You are my Father in Heaven. You created me in Your image.

> Therefore, it is my inheritance to be abundant with children.

I ask You to completely heal in me what is lacking, cursed, or wounded. I ask for a miracle in my reproductive systems, El Yalad. Male sterility breaks off my life in Jesus's Name. I rebuke low sperm count, poor sperm quality, sexually transmitted diseases, structural blockages, sexual dysfunctions and/or infections, hormonal imbalances, genetic disorders, and any other factor that would contribute to sterility. I speak to my penis, testicles, scrotum, epididymis, ducts, urethra, prostate gland, and vas deferens and command them to be healthy, whole, and healed.

You bless my loins to be fruitful. I am fertile. I am not barren, childless, or sterile. I decree that I am blessed because my quiver will be full of children.

As I meditate on and gratefully eat Your Flesh and drink Your Blood, I abide in You and You in me. I remember and honor Your selfless sacrifice by observing communion.

Triumphantly, I claim, receive, and apply the blessing that barrenness breaks and fruitfulness fills my life because that is what You paid for. May You receive the reward of Your suffering, my King. With thanks, joy, and faith, I appropriate Your brutalized Body and healing Blood. I love You. Thank You, Jesus, for **Our Holy Covenant.**

EL YALAD DECLARES

I am faithful. What I did for others, I can and will do for you. I endured the cross to break every wicked curse. So, understand that infertility is no match for My power.

I am the God who created you and am more than able to heal you so that you can be productive and fruitful. Rejoice with singing! Burst into a song of joy and a shout of praise, for increase is coming!

My Spirit hovers over every part of your reproductive system, releasing healing.

Even while you sleep, I am making you whole. Rest in Me. Do not labor for this promise. It is My delight to give you the desires of your heart.

Listen to Me. My report is accurate; believe it. Do not align or agree with the negative medical reports or word curses. Instead, cancel them, rewrite your story, and include My wonder-working power. I have broken the generational curse of barrenness off your bloodline. I have saved and healed you from every disease, infirmity, past sin, or dysfunction that could hinder your ability to produce. You are free and healed to procreate! I am Your Creator and My stripes have healed you. Write about that.

Take a deep breath. I remove all the stress, worry, and shame from you. Take another deep breath. I rebuke hope deferred, disappointment, and depression from your emotions. Instead, I fill you with hope, faith, and great expectancy. It is time for you to expect to be expecting!

Say it aloud and agree with Me,
"I expect to be expecting!"

As you speak My words out loud, let them sink in and let the healing begin.

Now, advance forward and enforce My triumph, which My Body and Blood purchased for you. My sacrifice on the cross secured everything you need.

I am El Yalad, the God Who Births, enabling you to multiply and fill the earth because this is your portion. This is your inheritance from Me. I break barrenness and make you fruitful. This is My promise to you sealed by **Our Holy Covenant.**

Scripture references—Genesis 1, Genesis 2, Deuteronomy 7, Psalm 113, Psalm 127, Psalm 31, John 6, Isaiah 54

Visit www.amandahill.org or scan the QR code below. Partake of the elements and then listen to the worship song that coincides with Day #16.

TASTE AND SEE

Did this day resonate with you and minister healing to you? If yes, be sure to recall, reflect, and record your healing journey.

If you answered no to the above question, do you know someone who struggles with infertility? Did you pray this prayer for them? If so, reach out to them today. Encourage them and let them know you are praying for them!

DAY 17

JOY, ENCOURAGEMENT, AND STRENGTH

2 CHRONICLES 30:21, EZRA 6:22, ACTS 2:46, ACTS 27:35-36

EL SIMCHAT-GILI, God My Exceeding Joy

EL SIMCHAT-GILI DECLARES

My grace is always more than enough for you. My power is fully expressed through your weaknesses. So, celebrate your weaknesses, for when you are weak, that is when I manifest My mighty power. It courses through your very being.

Come with Me, and let Me show you the path of life. In My Presence, there is fullness of joy; at My right hand, there are pleasures forevermore.

Grief and depression are not your portion from Me. I have given you beauty for ashes, the oil of joy for mourning, the garment of praise for the spirit of heaviness. Make the exchange with Me. Take off the old garment. My joy is your strength and your stronghold.

I know that you love Me passionately, although you have not seen Me with your physical eyes. Your belief and trust in Me saturate you with ecstatic, unspeakable joy, immersed in divine glory.

I delight in your songs of praise, offered in gratitude at the mention of My Name. My anger lasts just a moment, but My favor remains forever. Dear one, you may weep through the night, but remember that at daybreak, those tears will be transformed into shouts of joyful celebration!

My Kingdom is not about eating and drinking; it consists of righteousness, peace, and joy in My Spirit. I am in your midst as a Warrior Who saves. I rejoice over you with great joy and calm you with My love. I celebrate you with shouts of joy! I am the God of all hope, filling you with joy and peace because you trust in Me. As a result, you will overflow with confident hope through the power of My Spirit.

I am the Everlasting God, the Lord and Creator of the ends of the earth.

No one is equal to Me. I never tire or become weary. I am never confused or lacking in power. It delights Me to give you strength when you are fatigued. I increase your power when you are weak, providing ever-increasing strength. Even young people may faint and become exhausted; strong men may stumble and fall. But when you intertwine your heart with Mine, when you seek Me and wait for Me, I will renew your strength and fill you with mighty power. You will soar on wings like eagles, rising toward the sun. You will run and not grow weary; you will walk and never grow tired.

Now, advance forward and enforce My triumph, which My Body and Blood purchased for you. My sacrifice on the cross secured everything you need.

I am El Simchat-Gili, God Your Exceeding Joy Who infuses you with joy, encouragement, and strength! This is your inheritance from Me. I will give you joy, encouragement, and strength! I am your joy! I am your encouragement! I am your strength! This is My promise to you sealed by **Our Holy Covenant.**

I REPLY

Thank You, Jesus, for Your sacrifice. I remember and meditate on the price You paid for me. The New Covenant, purchased by Your Body and Blood, serves as my weapon for warring triumphantly. In humility, I confess my sins and ask for Your forgiveness. In Your mercy, cleanse my heart, mind, words, behavior, and anything that contradicts Your character and Holy Spirit. Acquit me of my unconscious, unintended faults. According to the greatness of Your compassion, blot out my transgressions. Wash me thoroughly from my wickedness, guilt, and iniquity.

I receive Your promise of joy, encouragement, and strength in my life through Your Body and Blood!

I know how to get along and live humbly because I have endured difficult times. In any and every circumstance, I have learned and am learning the secret of overcoming all things. I can do everything You have called me to do through You because You strengthen and empower me. I am self-sufficient in Your sufficiency.

You have made this day, and I choose to rejoice and be glad in it! I will find joy in You because You have made me glad. I am filled to overflowing with Your joy and delight. I can accomplish everything You have called me to because You strengthen and empower me to fulfill Your purposes. I experience unspeakable joy when I am with You. All my discouragement and hopelessness wash away, for Your joy is contagious and it strengthens me. Despair and darkness flee from me. When I am with You, I laugh and smile; I feel free. In Your presence, I release my need to control.

My heart is happy, which is good medicine, and my mind is filled with joy, which brings healing.

I will be joyful and will not stop praying. I will be thankful to You no matter what happens. This is the way You want me to live because my life belongs to You.

You are my refuge and strength, a very present and steadfast help in trouble. Therefore, I will not fear if the earth should change and the mountains shake and fall into the heart of the seas. There is a river whose streams make glad the city of God.

Partaking of Your tortured Body and shed Blood causes a rushing river of joy, encouragement, and strength to flood my heart, and I cannot help but rejoice!

Your fruit, the fruit of Your Spirit within me, is growing. Thank You for Unfailing Love, Overflowing Joy, Invincible Peace, Enduring Patience, Relentless Kindness, Abiding Goodness, Overcoming Faithfulness, Tangible Gentleness, and Steadfast Self-Control.

The promise You made to me has taken root in my heart. You take my ashes and turn them into a crown of beauty. You gather my tears of mourning and give me the oil of blissful joy and gladness. You give me a mantle of extravagant praise and discard my garment of heaviness of failure and fear.

There is nothing on earth I desire besides You. I may fail, but You are my rock and the strength of my heart and my portion forever.

As I meditate on and gratefully eat Your Flesh and drink Your Blood, I abide in You and You in me. I remember and honor Your selfless sacrifice by observing communion.

Triumphantly, I claim, receive, and apply the blessing of boundless grace and unmerited favor in my life because that is what You paid for. May You receive the reward of Your suffering, my King. With thanks, joy, and faith, I appropriate Your scourged Body and justifying Blood. I love You. Thank You, Jesus, for **Our Holy Covenant.**

Scripture references—Psalm 16, 2 Corinthians 12, Galatians 5, Psalm 73, 1 Peter 1, Romans 14, Zephaniah 3, Psalm 118, 1 Thessalonians 5, Nehemiah 8, Proverbs 17, Psalm 116, Romans 15, John 15, Psalm 46, Isaiah 40, John 6

Visit www.amandahill.org or scan the QR code below. Partake of the elements and then listen to the worship song that coincides with Day #17.

TASTE AND SEE

Has your joy, encouragement, or strength been depleted in the last season? If yes, ask Holy Spirit to help you identify the root causes.

Be intentional about worshipping throughout the day. Journal what transpires, noting when your joy, encouragement, and strength increase.

DAY 18

INTIMACY WITH JESUS

JOHN 13:23

ELOHIM AHAVAH, The God Who Loves

ELOHIM AHAVAH INITIATES

There is nothing I would not do for you. Do you believe Me? You are so deeply loved that I offered My own Body and Blood to save you. Your name is carved upon My heart and engraved on the palm of My hand.

Because of My sacrifice, you stand redeemed and whole, wearing clean garments instead of filthy rags. I desired to do this for you. You are worth My sacrifice. I have loved you with an everlasting love and have drawn you to Me, remaining faithful to you.

I am a Jealous lover. Do not lean on anyone but Me.

When you rest on and in Me, you can hear
the rhythm of My heartbeat.

That is when your heart syncs with Mine, keeping you in the right tempo and alignment with Me. Intimacy with Me ensures your timing is never early or late, but in pace with My movements.

When you rest on and in Me, you can hear Me
whisper My secrets to you.

I share My mysteries with My lovers, so they are never caught off guard or unaware. Intimacy with Me protects you from surprise attacks from the enemy.

When you rest on and in Me, My
fragrance rubs off on you.

Those who love My presence draw close to Me. Come and get closer still, then you will smell like My scent, My essence, and anointing. Intimacy with Me ensures you function and flow out of my divine direction, not from a religious paradigm.

When you rest on and in Me, I lead you up from
and out of the wilderness.

That season has passed. Do not return to that place. It is not your home. I Am. Intimacy with Me ensures that your wilderness stay is just a season and not a sentence.

Will you come away with Me? I am calling your name. Can you hear My Voice?

Now, advance forward and enforce My triumph, which My Body and Blood purchased for you. My sacrifice on the cross secured everything you need.

I Am Elohim Ahavah, the God Who Loves! This is your inheritance from Me. I have loved you. I do love you. I will always love you. This is My promise to you sealed by **Our Holy Covenant.**

I RESPOND

Thank You, Jesus, for Your sacrifice. I remember and meditate on the price You paid for me. The New Covenant, purchased by Your Body and Blood, serves as my weapon for warring triumphantly. In humility, I confess my sins and ask for Your forgiveness. In Your mercy, cleanse my heart, mind, words, behavior, and anything that contradicts Your character and Holy Spirit. Acquit me of my unconscious, unintended faults. According to the greatness of Your compassion, blot out my transgressions. Wash me thoroughly from my wickedness, guilt, and iniquity.

I receive Your promise of intimacy with You, Jesus, my Bridegroom through Your Body and Blood!

Forgive me for the times when my white hot, passionate love for You has cooled and become lukewarm. Apathy gained a foothold in my heart as I took my gaze off You. Forgive me, Jesus. I became distracted by the world and my flesh. Rekindle my passion for You, Jesus. Let the fire of Your Presence burn away my complacency, compromise, and convenience.

When I think of Your holy sacrifice for me, it overwhelms my heart. I long to fall more deeply in love with You. Untame my heart; let me love You freely and without restraint.

Forgive me for the other lovers I have leaned on. I was foolish and selfish. I recognize You as my Bridegroom, the One my heart adores, the One I need, and the only One who can satisfy me. I am ruined for any other lover; they all pale compared to You. I have tasted of Your goodness, and Your love is better than life itself. I choose to be a devoted Bride, no longer a distracted bystander.

Jesus, You are the center of my life.

You are the meaning in my life. You are the epitome of love. You sent Jesus, Your only Son, into the world so that I might live through Him. He is the propitiation, the satisfying offering for my sins. What kind of love is this? It is life changing! It is more than I can comprehend.

There is no fear in Your love. Your perfect love has driven out all fear. Thank You for this beautiful promise. I love You, but You loved me first. Holy Father, through the power of Your Spirit, teach me to love others with this same kind of love. May my love walk never grow cold. Keep me burning with Your passionate love, Elohim Ahavah!

Like John the Beloved, I desire to lean back on Your chest and hear Your heartbeat. I long to anoint Your feet with my tears, and break my alabaster box, pouring out my love on and for You. That is where I find my true place of holy authority. You are my everything.

Yes, I will come away with You.

You mean more than this world to me. You are beyond anything I could have ever dreamed of. You are the Lover of my soul. You are the Love of my life. I could never trade you for silver, gold, or indescribable riches. You are my treasure.

I look into Your fiery love-filled eyes, and I'm swept away!

As I meditate on and gratefully eat Your Flesh and drink Your Blood, I abide in You and You in me. I remember and honor Your selfless sacrifice by observing communion.

Triumphantly, I claim, receive, and apply the blessing of intimacy in my life because that is what You paid for. May You receive the reward of Your suffering, my King. With thanks, joy, and faith, I appropriate Your tortured Body and innocent Blood. I love You. Thank You, Jesus, for **Our Holy Covenant.**

Scripture references—Jeremiah 31:3, Song of Solomon 1–8, Psalm 27, John 6, 1 John 4

Visit www.amandahill.org or scan the QR code below. Partake of the elements and then listen to the worship song that coincides with Day #18.

TASTE AND SEE

Is it challenging for you to consider Jesus your Lover and Bridegroom? Whether yes or no, explore with Holy Spirit the reasons why you feel this way.

Be intentional over the next few days. Choose intimate worship songs, sing them to Him, and wait for His Presence. Be sure to journal your encounter.

DAY 19

DISCERNMENT

JOSHUA 7, MATTHEW 26:20–25, JOHN 13:21–30

ADONAI ORI, The Lord Is My Light

I BEGIN

Thank You, Jesus, for Your sacrifice. I remember and meditate on the price You paid for me. The New Covenant, purchased by Your Body and Blood, serves as my weapon for warring triumphantly. In humility, I confess my sins and ask for Your forgiveness. In Your mercy, cleanse my heart, mind, words, behavior, and anything that contradicts Your character and Holy Spirit. Acquit me of my unconscious, unintended faults. According to the greatness of Your compassion, blot out my transgressions. Wash me thoroughly from my wickedness, guilt, and iniquity.

I receive Your promise of discernment and discerning of spirits in my life through Your Body and Blood!

You are Adonai Ori and You are my Light. You know everything. There is nothing concealed that will not be disclosed, nor anything hidden that will not be made known. Thank You, Lord, that whatever is said in the dark will be heard in the light, and whatever has been whispered behind closed doors will be revealed. I welcome Your light to shine brightly in my life, for all things become visible when Your light exposes them, for it is Your light that makes everything visible.

I agree and align with Your Word and
declare, "Let there be light!"

I will not believe every spirit; instead, I test the spirits to see whether they are from You or another source. Every spirit acknowledging and confessing that Jesus has come in the flesh as a man, is from You, which I receive. However, any spirit that does not confess that Jesus came in the flesh and denies that You are the Son of God is the spirit of the antichrist, which I reject.

I choose to carefully test everything against the plumbline of Your Word so I can discern what is good versus almost good, truth versus almost truth, godly versus almost godly. I will hold firm to that which is good, true, and godly. Your Word is Truth. It can never lie. Therefore, I will measure all things in my life by and according to Your Word, for it is the standard. Discretion watches over me; understanding and discernment guard me to keep me from the way of evil and the people of evil.

As I sit at the table You have set for me, I feast on the meal You have prepared. Your Body is my true spiritual food, and Your Blood is my true spiritual drink. I abide in You and You abide in me, empowering me with discernment, allowing me to identify the betrayer who sits nearby. There is no "Judas" who can conceal their hidden motives from You.

> Jesus, tenderize and purify my heart so I will still love and serve the betrayer, washing his feet, just like You did.

I decree that my spiritual senses are opened to another heightened realm when I eat the bread and drink from the cup. I speak to my sight, hearing, smell, taste, and touch and command an intensification and a more accurate level of discernment. Senses, you will come alive to see, hear, smell, taste, and touch the Third Heaven in a more intense, authentic way.

Thank You, Adonai Ori, for helping me discern when I am being misused, manipulated, abused, prostituted, or exploited. I ask for rightly aligned relationships that will bless me, and I will bless them in return.

Likewise, show me my own heart. Help me discern when I am operating out of opportunism toward others. Holy Spirit, purify my heart. Let me treat others the way I want to be treated. I will guard my heart against selfish ambition and refuse to allow flattery to lead me into manipulating others for my own advancement.

Jesus, I ask that You baptize Your Church, Your Bride with supernatural discernment and discerning of spirits. Anoint us to distinguish sound, godly doctrine from the deceptive doctrine of man-made religions, deceitful and seductive spirits, and the doctrine of demons. Sharpen our senses, Holy Spirit!

Let us also discern how, when, where, and why the enemy is moving and strategizing. Grant Your Body the ability to see the "Achan" in our midst before disaster strikes so we do not lose battles we should win. Help us know and correctly identify those laboring among us and warring beside us. Let us never elevate and prioritize gifts over fruit, entertainment over anointing, or charisma over character.

Give us eyes that comprehend, ears that understand, and hearts that know You.

As I meditate on and gratefully eat Your Flesh and drink Your Blood, I abide in You and You in me. I remember and honor Your selfless sacrifice by observing communion.

Triumphantly, I claim, receive, and apply the blessing of sharp discernment in my life because that is what You paid for. May You receive the reward of Your suffering, my King. With thanks, joy, and faith, I appropriate Your crucified Body and consecrated Blood. I love You. Thank You, Jesus, for **Our Holy Covenant.**

ADONAI ORI RESPONDS

When you share in My sacrifice, you become more aware of who I Am and who you are because of Me. This beautiful spiritual transaction trades your sight for My sight, your hearing for My hearing, your smell for My smell, your taste for My taste, and your touch for My touch. When My Spirit infuses your senses, nothing can hide.

Remain teachable, abiding in My Word and submitted to My Spirit, and you will not be deceived. I will give you clarity and focus so that you can rightly judge what is from Me and what is from the enemy.

Now, advance forward and enforce My triumph, which My Body and Blood purchased for you. My sacrifice on the cross secured everything you need.

I am Adonai Ori, the Lord Your Light, Who favors you with sharp discernment because that is what You asked of Me! This is your inheritance from Me. You are discerning. This is My promise to you sealed by **Our Holy Covenant.**

Scripture references—Luke 12, Ephesians 5, 1 John 4, Proverbs 2, John 6, Psalm 27, 1 Corinthians 12, 1 Timothy 4, 1 Thessalonians 5, Isaiah 6, Jeremiah 24

Visit www.amandahill.org or scan the QR code below. Partake of the elements and then listen to the worship song that coincides with Day #19.

TASTE AND SEE

Have you ever been in a room with someone, knowing you could not trust their motives? Were you able to love and serve them like Jesus did with Judas?

The Lord desires for you to see what He sees and hear what He hears. Over the next several days, take time to recognize how your senses are shifting since observing communion. Be sure to journal your experiences.

DAY 20

NATIONAL REFORMATION AND SPIRITUAL AWAKENING

2 KINGS 23:21–25, 2 CHRONICLES 30:13–31, 2 CHRONICLES 31–32, 2 CHRONICLES 35:1–19

MELEKH HAGOYIM, King of Nations

THE EKKLESIA INITIATES

Thank You, Jesus, for Your sacrifice. We remember and meditate on the price You paid for us, Your Bride, Your Ekklesia. The New Covenant, purchased by Your Body and Blood, serves as our weapons for warring triumphantly. In humility, we confess the sins of Your Church and ask for Your forgiveness. In Your mercy, cleanse our hearts, minds, words, behaviors, and anything that contradicts Your character and Holy Spirit. Acquit us of our unconscious, unintended faults. According to the greatness of Your compassion, blot out our transgressions. Wash us thoroughly from our wickedness, transgressions, and iniquities.

We receive Your promise of national reformation
and spiritual awakening for our nation
through Your Body and Blood!

We are Your people, called by Your Name. Holy Lord, we humble ourselves, pray, seek Your face, and turn from our wicked ways. Hear us from Heaven, forgive our sins, and heal our land!

We stand as intercessors on behalf of our nation. We repent for the sins of our ancestors and this generation. Please forgive us of our pride, greed, wrath, envy, lust, gluttony, and slothfulness. Although we, as a nation, may not seem to be serving You now, Lord, a remnant is rising, and we will not stop pleading for the soul of this nation! We decree that we will serve You wholeheartedly, and in return, we will be blessed, prosperous, and favored by You. You have chosen us as Your inheritance.

We decree that this nation is turning to You, the One true God. We have chosen to serve You, Great King! We receive and embrace Your Word, ways, precepts, and truth. May Your holy, reverential fear visit every household and convict us of our sins. Lord, invade our nation!

Let mercy triumph over judgment.

With a single breath, You frustrate the plans and scatter the schemes of the nations that oppose You. You make their thoughts and plans ineffective and unsuccessful, while Your plans remain firm throughout all generations. Your purposes can never be shaken nor can they fail.

We serve notice to the enemy now. We renounce and revoke every demonic agreement, deceptive oath, and illegal covenant that was made with Satan and his dark kingdom and our nation. We divorce and break all vows with the enemy. We are married, as one, to our Maker; King Jesus is our husband, the Commander of Angel Armies. He is this nation's Kinsman-Redeemer, the Holy One of Israel. He is the Mighty God of all the earth!

Protect Your Ekklesia from political and religious persecution, Lord. As Your Kingdom representatives in the earth realm, we prohibit the government and its judicial system from being used as a weapon to oppress believers and infringe upon their religious liberties.

Righteousness and justice are the foundation of Your throne. May Your throne be established upon the hearts and minds of those who hold governmental offices. Expose corruption, foul play, deception, and lies, Holy Spirit! Pull back the covers on every evil deed, satanic network, back-room deal, undercover agenda, and pay-to-play agreement. Let justice run down like a raging river and righteousness like an ever-flowing, abundant stream.

We decree that godly leaders from the greatest to the least will carry Your Presence and lead this nation as the Spirit of the Lord rests on them—the Spirit of wisdom, and understanding, the Spirit of counsel and strength, the Spirit of knowledge, and the reverential and obedient fear of the Lord! When the godly are in leadership, the people rejoice. Holy Spirit, quickly deliver us from the oppression of the ungodly.

Release Your fire, Lord, and burn up all that is not of You. We sever the enemy's puppet strings of control and manipulation. Jezebel is thrown out the window, and the sword of the Lord beheads her false prophets and wicked priests. May the occultic blood sacrifices that have empowered principalities, powers, rulers of darkness, and spiritual wickedness in high places lose their controlling power now.

The Blood of the Passover Lamb triumphs over any other blood sacrifice.

So, we now freshly apply the Blood of Jesus over the doors and gates of this nation! No weapon that is formed against our nation may prosper or succeed. Every tongue that rises against us in judgment shall be condemned. This peace and security in the face of opposition is our heritage from You, Lord, because we belong to You. This is our vindication from You!

Your Bride is a unified army and we ascend to the high places of this nation, dismantling and annihilating the enemy's thrones of iniquity.

We tear down the altars of every false god, and we build the altar of prayer and worship to King Jesus! We command the portals of Hell to close and the portals of God to open. The gates of Hell will not prevail against this nation. We possess the keys of the Kingdom of God to reclaim and restore the territory that the enemy has stolen.

In Your Name, King Jesus, we erect a wall of fire to surround and protect this nation. We deploy angelic intervention and assistance now. We bind and rebuke all sleeper cells, religious terrorists, and demons of Islamic jihad now. We declare that Allah is not the god of our nation. We forbid violence and bloodthirsty people within our borders.

Let every undercover one-world agenda and destructive conspiracy be exposed. We forbid lawlessness, secular humanism, anti-Semitism, and antichrist spirits from rising and ruling in our nation.

King of kings, shake all spheres of society, the mountains of influence in my nation: family, religion, government, media, arts/entertainment, business, and education. May these structures be filled and governed by the devout disciples of King Jesus.

Just as Israel experienced great spiritual revival and national reformation after Hezekiah and Josiah celebrated Passover, we cry out for the same encounter! As we honor and remember Your sacrifice through observing communion, we intercede with fasting and prayer for revival in Your Church, spiritual awakening in Your people, and supernatural reformation in our nation! We thank You in advance that You, Melekh Hagoyim, are coming to pour out Your Spirit on our nation! We will not place any restraints or restrictions on how, where, or when You come—just come!

As we meditate on and gratefully eat Your Flesh and drink Your Blood, we abide in You and You in us. We remember and honor Your selfless sacrifice by observing communion.

Triumphantly, we claim, receive, and apply the blessing of national reformation and spiritual awakening in this nation because that is what You paid for. May You receive the reward of Your suffering, our King. With thanks, joy, and faith, we appropriate Your bruised Body and redemptive Blood. We love You. Thank You, Jesus, for **Our Holy Covenant.**

MELEKH HAGOYIM DECREES

When nations rise up and plot against Me, I sit on My throne and laugh at their rebellion. Nothing they do will succeed or endure.

I am working even in your nation. Stop dwelling on the past, rehearsing old mistakes. Choose not to remember the former things. Listen to Me carefully: I am about to do a brand-new thing. Even now, it is sprouting, growing, and maturing. Do you not see it? Do you not perceive it? I will make a way in the wilderness. I am the God who opens up flowing streams in the desert.

Indeed, I have birthed a nation in a day, suddenly bringing them forth as a people. So, yes, I can certainly and effortlessly effect significant change to and in your nation. Cry aloud and do not hold back! Lift up your voice like a trumpet for your nation. I am coming with My fire, and wind! All you have asked, I will do. The nations of the earth belong to Me. They are my inheritance from My Father.

Now, advance forward and enforce My triumph, which My Body and Blood purchased for you. My sacrifice on the cross secured everything you need.

I am Melekh Hagoyim, King of Nations! This is your inheritance from Me. I will give you national reformation and spiritual awakening. This is My promise to you sealed by **Our Holy Covenant.**

Scripture references—Isaiah 11, 2 Corinthians 12, Ephesians 6, 2 Kings 18, Amos 4, Isaiah 54, 2 Chronicles 7, Isaiah 58, Psalm 2, Matthew 16, 2 Kings 9, Psalm 89

Visit www.amandahill.org or scan the QR code below. Partake of the elements and then listen to the worship song that coincides with Day #20.

TASTE AND SEE

Research the prophetic promises over your nation. In faith, speak those promises back to the Lord and remind Him of His Word.

What reforms need to take place in your nation? How can you partner with the Lord to see this manifest? Ask Holy Spirit to direct your intercession and journal what He speaks.

DAY 21

MIRACLES

EXODUS 14:13–31, JOSHUA 24:17, ACTS 2:42–43

ADONAI LO SHANAH,
The Lord Who Does Not Change

ADONAI LO SHANAH BEGINS

I am the One true and living God—eternal and unchanging. I am the Alpha and the Omega, the first and the last, the beginning and the end. I am the One who was, who is, and who is to come. I am the Ageless, Timeless Ancient of Days.

I perform miracles that reflect My divine nature. What I did for My people, Israel, was simple, easy, and effortless for Me, flowing from My boundless power and love. Miracles are a part of My nature. I am the miracle-working God. What I did for them, I long to do for you! I have never changed.

I call Myself "The Lord Who Does Not Change" because I am the same yesterday, today, and forever.

I have done, am doing, and will continue to do things you have never heard of before. Things that are beyond your ability to imagine. These are things that no ear has ever heard, nor has any eye ever witnessed. I am Majesty itself, and no other god can even come close to Me.

I reign as the sovereign King over all the earth, and My dominion stretches endlessly into eternity. A shroud of clouds and thick, deep darkness surround Me. My magnificent throne of glory rests upon a foundation of unwavering righteousness and unyielding justice. Fiery flames surge before Me, consuming My adversaries on every side. My lightning bursts forth, illuminating the entire earth with its blinding brilliance, causing the ground itself to tremble and shake. The mighty mountains melt away like wax under the intensity of My burning Presence.

Can you perceive how powerful I am?

I worked miracles then, I work miracles now, and I will forever work miracles. I am the miracle-working God! Throughout the ages, I have woven miracles into the very fabric of life—turning ordinary water into exquisite wine, healing the broken and the weary, and even raising those ensnared by death back to the light of life. My capacity to work wonders is not confined to ancient tales; I continue to manifest miracles in the world around you. I breathe, and miracles manifest.

Miracles took place through the hands of My devoted servants: Moses, with his staff parting the raging sea; Elijah, who called down fire from

Heaven; Elisha, bringing the dead back to life; Esther, who bravely saved her people; Gideon, overcoming insurmountable odds; David, the shepherd who defeated giants; Jael, with her swift courage; and the apostles Peter, John, and Paul, who proclaimed My Name and healed the sick.

Those who honor and partake of My Body and Blood have the authority to work extraordinary miracles beyond human capability, which manifests My power.

I can do anything. My power is limitless. What kind of miracle do you need from Me? Ask Me! Ask and keep on asking, and it will be given to you; seek and keep on seeking, and you will find; knock and keep on knocking, and the door will open. For if you persistently ask, you will receive. If you remain steadfast in your seeking, you will find. And if you continue to knock, doors of opportunity will open to you.

I am perfect, so I know how to give good and advantageous gifts to My children Who earnestly ask Me.

So, now, ask Me. Tell Me what miracle you need. I am here. I intervene for those who patiently wait and long for Me.

Now, advance forward and enforce My triumph, which My Body and Blood purchased for you. My sacrifice on the cross secured everything you need.

I am Adonai Lo Shanah, the Lord Who Does Not Change! This is your inheritance from Me. I will give you miracles, miracles, miracles! This is My promise to you sealed by **Our Holy Covenant.**

I REPLY

Thank You, Jesus, for Your sacrifice. I remember and meditate on the price You paid for me. The New Covenant, purchased by Your Body and Blood, serves as my weapon for warring triumphantly. In humility, I confess my sins and ask for Your forgiveness. In Your mercy, cleanse my heart, mind, words, behavior, and anything that contradicts Your character and Holy Spirit. Acquit me of my unconscious, unintended faults. According to the greatness of Your compassion, blot out my transgressions. Wash me thoroughly from my wickedness, guilt, and iniquity.

I receive Your promise of miracles in my life through Your Body and Blood!

Adonai Lo Shanah, I marvel at Your mighty miracles; each one is a testament to Your greatness. You are the Famous One, and my heart is filled with reverence for You.

I have read Your Word, and I know the things that made You renowned. I am stunned when I consider Your miracles. Oh, Lord, do them again in our day! Let my generation experience, as firsthand witnesses, Your mighty miracles and Your supernatural deeds!

There is nothing too difficult for You!

You created the world in six days.
You gave Abraham and Sarah a son.
You judged Egypt with the ten plagues.
You parted the Red Sea for Moses and rescued Your people.
You provided manna from Heaven and poured water from a rock.
You stopped the sun's movement for Joshua and the Israelites.
You caused a donkey to speak in a human voice to Balaam.
You empowered David to kill a lion, a bear, and a giant.
You sent fire from Heaven to consume Elijah's sacrifice.
You multiplied the widow's oil.
You brought Your people back to their homeland, Israel.
You delivered Daniel from a den of lions and the three Hebrew boys from the fiery furnace.
You preserved Jonah in the belly of a great fish.
You turned water into wine.
You healed the sick.
You raised the dead.
You caused fish to appear suddenly for a miraculous catch.
You calmed the storm on the sea.
You cast six thousand demons into pigs.
You multiplied bread for nearly twenty thousand people.
You walked on the water.
You caused the blind to see and the deaf to hear.
You worked miracles because You are the Miracle-Working God!

I remember. I remember what You have done. You performed all these miracles, and You still work miracles today! You are the Miracle-Working, unchanging God!

Forgive me for forgetting Who You are.

I have acted as one who does not believe or know You. My faith has wavered. I repent! Forgive my unbelief. I break the back of the spirit of unbelief that causes me to only believe and trust in what I can see!

I revoke and renounce my agreement with doubt and unbelief. I speak to my measure of faith and command it to grow!

I will diligently hear the Logos and Kairos Word of God! Once I hear Your Word, I will be intentional about believing what You have said. And then I will live what I have listened to and believed. Jesus, where my prayer life is lukewarm, set it on fire. I long to know You more deeply.

As I remember Your sacrifice, increase my measure of faith to become miracle-working faith, Holy Jesus. You have never changed, ever. What You performed back then, You will perform today. I not only want to witness these miracles with my eyes, but I also want to work unusual miracles through my hands. If You can use anyone, Lord, use me! I believe You are the God of Miracles!

Miracles are my portion!

As I meditate on and gratefully eat Your Flesh and drink Your Blood, I abide in You and You in me. I remember and honor Your selfless sacrifice by observing communion.

Triumphantly, I claim, receive, and apply the blessing of miracles in my life because that is what You paid for. May You receive the reward of Your suffering, my King. With thanks, joy, and faith, I appropriate Your beaten Body and powerful Blood. I love You. Thank You, Jesus, for **Our Holy Covenant.**

Scripture references—Isaiah 64, Psalm 97, Psalm 2, Isaiah 54, Habakkuk 3, Psalm 147, Matthew 7, Daniel 7, Romans 10, Genesis 1, Genesis 21, Exodus 7-12, Exodus 14, Exodus 16, Joshua 10, Numbers 22, 1 Samuel 17, 1 Kings 18, 2 Kings 4, Jeremiah 29, Daniel 6, Jonah 1, John 2, Matthew 4, John 11, Luke 5, Mark 4, Matthew 8, John 6, Matthew 14, Luke 7

Visit www.amandahill.org or scan the QR code below. Partake of the elements and then listen to the worship song that coincides with Day #21.

TASTE AND SEE

Reflect on the times you may have wrestled between trust and unbelief. What did you learn about the Lord's unchanging faithfulness?

Fasting has the power to break off unbelief from your prayer time and thought life. Ask Holy Spirit how you need to move forward with regular fasting to conquer your flesh and increase your spirit. Record what He says to you.

DAY 22

DIRECTION

EXODUS 13:17–22

ADONAI ROHI, The Lord My Shepherd

I BEGIN

Thank You, Jesus, for Your sacrifice. I remember and meditate on the price You paid for me. The New Covenant, purchased by Your Body and Blood, serves as my weapon for warring triumphantly. In humility, I confess my sins and ask for Your forgiveness. In Your mercy, cleanse my heart, mind, words, behavior, and anything that contradicts Your character and Holy Spirit. Acquit me of my unconscious, unintended faults. According to the greatness of Your compassion, blot out my transgressions. Wash me thoroughly from my wickedness, guilt, and iniquity.

I receive Your promise of direction in my life
through Your Body and Blood!

Adonai Rohi, just as You guided and shepherded Your people, Israel, with a pillar of cloud by day and a pillar of fire by night, so You also lead me in the direction I should go. I may not always understand your path for my life, but I trust in You. I trust in Your love and believe You want what is best for me.

I belong to You. My ear is tuned to hear Your voice. You call me by name and say, "This is the way; walk in it." I will only listen to You and will not be seduced or swayed by the voice of the thief. I know Your sound, Your movements, and Your call. You walk before me, and I follow You closely. Jesus, You came so that I may have and enjoy life in abundance, far more than I could ever expect.

Thank You for laying down Your life for me. You are the Good Shepherd, guiding me along my path.

Adonai Rohi, I welcome and submit to Your guidance and leadership. You guide me with Your watchful eyes, always observing my path with Your personalized divine counsel. I refuse to be like a difficult horse or a stubborn mule. I will not fight against or resist Your purpose, path, and plan for my life. Please take me to places I have never been before. You will not have to drag me along. I willingly submit to Your commands because I belong to You, and You know what is best for me.

I will not rely on my own opinions, insights, or understanding. Instead, in everything I do, in all my ways, thoughts, and behaviors, I will acknowledge and recognize You, Jesus. With all my heart, I place my faith in You to lead me. You will make my paths straight and smooth, removing any obstacles that block my way.

I welcome the Spirit of Truth to guide me fully and completely into all truth. Jesus, You are the only way to God. You are the true Truth and the living Life. No one comes to the Father except through You.

I ask You, Jesus, to let me know Your ways. Teach me Your paths. Guide me in Your truth and teach me, for You are the God of my salvation; for You and only You, I wait expectantly all day long.

You are my best friend, Adonai Rohi. I always have more than enough and lack nothing because You care for my every need. You allow me to lie down and rest in lush, green springtime pastures. You gently guide me to the still, quiet streams of serenity. It is here that You refresh, restore, and revive my soul. Tenderly, You lead me in the paths of righteousness so that I can bring honor and glory to Your Name. Even when Your path takes me through the sunless valley of deepest darkness, I refuse to fear anything.

I trust You are with me and will never leave or forsake me.

God of all comfort, You know exactly how to console me. You prepare a table before me in the presence of my enemies. You anoint me with the fragrance of Your Presence, and I am refreshed and drenched in oil. My cup abundantly overflows. Surely, Your great goodness, miraculous mercy, and lavish love will follow me all the days of my blessed life. I shall forever dwell all the days of my life in the house of the Lord.

I will run the way of Your commandments with purpose, for You have given me a willing heart. I love Your Word! It is a lamp to my feet and a light to my path.

I will not be conformed to this world with its superficial values and customs any longer, but I am being transformed and progressively changed by the renewing of my mind. Then, I may prove for myself what God's good, acceptable, and perfect will is for my life.

I have made many wrong turns in the past. Please, forgive me, Lord, for choosing my own way. Help me to recognize if I am on a misguided path—one of shame, pain, or any road that You have not laid out for me. Lead me back to Your glorious, everlasting way, as it is the path that brings me closer to Your heart.

As I meditate on and gratefully eat Your Flesh and drink Your Blood, I abide in You and You in me. I remember and honor Your selfless sacrifice by observing communion.

Triumphantly, I claim, receive, and apply the blessing of Your direction and guidance in my life because that is what You paid for. May You receive the reward of Your suffering, my King. With thanks, joy, and faith, I appropriate Your scourged Body and sacrificial shed Blood. I love You. Thank You, Jesus, for **Our Holy Covenant.**

ADONAI ROHI DECREES

I am the Good Shepherd, watching over you with unwavering and perfect care. When I say your name, You recognize My voice because you belong to Me. No one will ever snatch you from My hand. The Father has given you to Me, and He is the greatest and mightiest of all. Nothing and no one is able to snatch you out of Our Father's careful and loving hand.

The Father and I are One, and together We watch over you and hold you securely with tenderness.

I hold within My heart the beautiful plans and thoughts I have for your life. My intentions for you are rich with peace, overflowing with prosperity, and filled with the promise of well-being—never leading you into disaster or despair. I long to see you fulfill your future and be filled with hope.

Remember that My thoughts are not your thoughts. Nor are My ways your ways. As high as the heavens are above the earth, so My ways and My thoughts are higher than yours.

You have walked in righteousness; because of this, I have lovingly guided and firmly established your steps. Your journey delights Me, and in response, I have adorned your path with blessings. If you ever doubt the path you should take, turn your eyes upon Me, seeking My perfect will for you. I will shine My light on your way, ensuring your feet remain steady and preventing you from slipping or stumbling on your path.

Now, advance forward and enforce My triumph, which My Body and Blood purchased for you. My sacrifice on the cross secured everything you need.

I am Adonai Rohi, the Lord Your Shepherd, Who guides you because I love you! This is your inheritance from Me. I will direct you. This is My promise to you sealed by **Our Holy Covenant.**

Scripture references—Isaiah 30, Psalm 32, Proverbs 3, John 16, Psalm 25, Romans 12, Psalm 119, Psalm 139, Psalm 23, John 10, Jeremiah 29, Psalm 37, Isaiah 55, John 6

Visit www.amandahill.org or scan the QR code below. Partake of the elements and then listen to the worship song that coincides with Day #22.

TASTE AND SEE

Have you ever received clear direction from the Lord but chose to ignore it? If so, where did your choice to disregard His Voice leave you?

Is it challenging to trust Him in circumstances you do not understand? List three areas you have faced or are facing that do not make sense. Ask Holy Spirit for clarity. Ask Him for His thoughts and ways about those issues. Now, listen for His response.

DAY 23

WOMEN ARISE, ACTIVATE, AND ADVANCE

EXODUS 15:20, LUKE 24:1–12

SAHADI, My Advocate

SAHADI OPENS

Hear Me, My daughters, women who represent half of My Body. I am Sahadi, Your Advocate.

You are not second choice; I made you co-laborers.
You are not illegitimate; I validated you.
You are not difficult; I created you intricately.
You are not incapable; I empowered you.
You are not emotional; I designed you to nurture.
You are not disqualified; I authorized you.
You are not weak; I fashioned you resilient.

You are not captive; I untamed you.
You are not lacking; I formed you to prosper.
You are not broken; I healed you.
You are not inferior; I made you worthy.

Church, look at My example. I invited women into My circle and went out of My way to minister to them. I purposefully chose women to surround Me in My ministry and empowered them to carry My message. My disciples and I received financial support from women. At my crucifixion, burial, and resurrection, women were present when most of My disciples fled in fear.

I am not a misogynist; I am an Advocate of women. I shatter glass ceilings, break Pharisaical laws, and challenge traditional and religious customs.

My Word recognizes that women can be mothers, judges, queens, deacons, prophets, evangelists, teachers, entrepreneurs, inheritors, leaders, apostles, co-heirs, disciples, pastors, counselors, elders, authors, and warriors.

Some have used My Word as a prison to confine, restrict, and muzzle half of My army. This is not My heart, purpose, or intention. I need My whole army activated, mobilized, and engaged.

The first man, Adam, became a living soul; I, the last Adam, became a life-giving spirit. I broke every curse ever issued, including the one against My daughters.

I came to liberate and partner with women. Throughout history, we have united to change culture, save nations, and carry My Presence.

There is nothing the Ekklesia cannot achieve when My sons and daughters unite!

Mary carried and birthed My Son, Jesus, the Living Word, and so still today I mandate women to carry, deliver, teach, and preach the gospel, My written Word. This decree has not changed. Even today, I am activating women to carry and proclaim My message of truth.

My longest recorded conversation was with a woman named Photini, also known as the Samaritan Woman. She was the first person to whom I revealed Myself as the Messiah. After Our encounter at the well, she left and told the city about Me, and many believed because of her testimony. She was the first to preach about Me before My sacrifice on the cross.

Mary of Magdala was the first person I appeared to and spoke with after My death, burial, and resurrection. I directed her to go and tell My brothers, commissioning her to announce My triumph over death. She was the first to preach about Me after My sacrifice on the cross.

So even now, I reveal Myself to My daughters, calling them to arise, mantling them to go, teach, and preach.

Look at My list of chosen vessels: Eve, Sarah, Hagar, Rahab, Esther, Rebekah, Abigail, Deborah, Tryphosa, Mary, Naomi, Rachel, Persis, Jael, Leah, Photini, Phoebe, Junia, Priscilla, Nympha, Prisca, Lydia,

Ruth, Mary Magdalene, Tryphena, Miriam, Elizabeth, Mary of Bethany, Martha, Hannah, Bathsheba, Anna, Euodia, Syntyche, Tamar, Jochebed, Shifra, Puah, Zipporah, Jonna, Susanna, Salome, Lois, and Eunice.

Hear Me, My daughters. I am Sahadi, Your Advocate. Your Champion. Your Supporter. Your Promoter. Your Backer. Your Partner.

It is time for you to understand that if I am for you, who could ever stand against you? If you have felt overlooked, rejected, and treated unfairly, allow your heart to be healed from those wounds. Do not allow offense to take root and grow into bitterness. Forgive and bless the ones who hurt you and then arise, be activated and advance!

The serpent hates you. You are a threat to his plans. In the Garden of Eden, I decreed that your hostility, your hatred against him would be My weapon to terrorize his kingdom. You identify and expose the enemy as a deceiver. You terrify him, and it delights Me and causes great laughter! I fashioned you to be My unique, surprising, courageous, triumphant instrument of destruction against Hell.

All of the kingdom of Hell fears that you will realize how powerful and essential you are to My end-time plans. That is why it has twisted My Word and formed weapons against you. Hell knows what you possess. You are a devil-exposing, snake-stomping, truth-carrying, purpose-fulfilling, faith-believing, fire-imparting, gospel-preaching, Holy Ghost-anointed daughter of the King.

My submission to My Father's plan tore the veil of the Holy of Holies in the temple from top to bottom, shaking the earth, splitting rocks, opening tombs, and resurrecting the dead. My sacrifice also destroyed the dividing wall between Jew and Greek, slaves and free, male and female. Those who believe are all one in Me, and no one can claim spiritual superiority. There is no distinction.

Where My Spirit is, there is liberty, a complete emancipation from bondage. It is time for there to be true freedom in My Body!

When you partake of My torn Body and holy Blood, My Spirit awakens passion and captures the hearts of My female vessels, releasing and empowering them to fulfill the call I have mandated.

Now, advance forward and enforce My triumph, which My Body and Blood purchased for you. My sacrifice on the cross secured everything you need.

I am Sahadi, Your Advocate because you are favored by Me! This is your inheritance from Me. I will arise, activate, and advance you, My daughters! This is My promise to you sealed by **Our Holy Covenant.**

THE EKKLESIA RESPONDS

Thank You, Jesus, for Your sacrifice. We remember and meditate on the price You paid for us, Your Bride. The New Covenant, purchased by Your Body and Blood, serves as our weapons for warring triumphantly. In humility, we confess the sins of Your Church and ask for Your forgiveness. In Your mercy, cleanse our hearts, minds, words, behaviors, and anything that contradicts Your character and Holy Spirit. Acquit us of our unconscious, unintended faults. According to the greatness of Your compassion, blot out our transgressions. Wash us thoroughly from our wickedness, transgressions, and iniquities.

We receive Your promise of women arising, activating, and advancing in the earth through Your Body and Blood!

The spirit of religion, disguised as order, has suffocated the lives and robbed the destinies of Your daughters. We reject the lies, behaviors, and thought processes associated with secular feminism, as well as the spirits of Jezebel, Delilah, Herodias, Athaliah, Sapphira, and Potiphar's wife. Your women are pure and godly and know how to honor others well. They act justly, love mercy, and walk humbly.

Forgive us, Your Ekklesia, for partnering with and agreeing with these deceptive falsehoods and demeaning fabrications against Your daughters. We have wrongly imposed limitations on the other half of Your army due to preconceived ideas, jealous motives, and manmade doctrines. Jesus, please redeem the time that has been lost due to our errors. We will support, not suppress, champion, not control, release, not restrict, and love, not limit, the women who are arising, activating, and advancing.

Come and transform our religious paradigms into new wine paradigms, Holy Spirit!

You, Awesome God, give the command, and the warring women of Zion who proclaim and preach the good news are a great army! Thank You for promising to pour out Your Spirit on all flesh: sons and daughters will prophesy, old men will dream dreams, and young men will see visions. You will pour out Your Spirit even on the male and female servants. You are faithful to fulfill what You have promised. We agree with Your covenant of hope, bringing equality for all who are found in You!

Father, as Your representatives in the earth realm, we repent for allowing and submitting to the double standards against Your daughters, which are biblically erroneous. We have accepted the lies fed to us by the enemy, but no more! We recognize the need for the whole army to be ignited, emboldened, and marching together, side by side.

We, Your Ekklesia, Your reigning, ruling, governing, legislating Body in the earth realm thank You for men and women, walking side by side in authority, honor, humility, and the fear of the Lord.

As we meditate on and gratefully eat Your Flesh and drink Your Blood, we abide in You and You in us. We remember and honor Your selfless sacrifice by observing communion.

Triumphantly, we claim, receive, and apply the blessing of women arising, activating, and advancing because that is what You paid for. May You receive the reward of Your suffering, our King. With thanks, joy, and faith, we appropriate Your suffered Body and spotless Blood. We love You. Thank You, Jesus, for **Our Holy Covenant.**

Scripture references—Genesis 3, 1 Corinthians 15, Galatians 3, Matthew 27, Romans 3, Joel 2, Micah 6, Psalm 68, Romans 8

Visit www.amandahill.org or scan the QR code below. Partake of the elements and then listen to the worship song that coincides with Day #23.

TASTE AND SEE

Have you witnessed or personally experienced women in the Body of Christ being overlooked? Did this concern you, or is it a common occurrence?

After reading today's chapter, was there any shift in your perspective regarding women in leadership? Is there anything you could do to better support women in their leadership roles?

DAY 24

TRIUMPH OVER THE ENEMY

EXODUS 14:24–28, EXODUS 17:8–16, EXODUS 23:27–33, NUMBERS 33:3–4, JOSHUA 10

ADONAI NISSI, The Lord Is My Banner

ADONAI NISSI INITIATES

I have never been defeated. Take a moment to reflect on this truth: It is impossible for Me to lose. Never. Ever.

I disarmed all supernatural rulers, authorities, and forces of evil that were against you. I made a public spectacle of all the powers and principalities of darkness, stripping them of their weapons, powers, and spiritual authority to accuse you. Through the power of the cross, I led them in a triumphal procession as My prisoners. I was not their prisoner; they were Mine!

Your enemies are My enemies.

Remember that flesh and blood are not your actual adversaries. You are not fighting against physical opponents; your struggle is against rulers, powers, the world forces of this present darkness, and the spiritual forces of wickedness in the heavenly places.

Your armor comes from Me, and with it, you can successfully resist and stand your ground, fully prepared, completely immovable, and ultimately triumphant!

So, stand firm. Be sure to tighten the belt of truth around your waist and put on the breastplate of righteousness. Strap on your feet the readiness that comes from the gospel of peace. Above all, lift up the protective shield of faith, with which you will extinguish all the flaming arrows of the evil one. Put on the helmet of salvation and take up the sword of the Spirit, which is the Word of God. Nothing can stand against you.

I am Your Rock, Shield, and great strength, who trains your hands for war and your fingers for battle. I am Your fortress, high tower, and Rescuer. I subdue nations before you.

I flash lightning and scatter your enemies. I send out My arrows and confuse, reroute, embarrass, and frustrate them into defeat.

I am Adonai Nissi, and I send
confusion into your enemy's camp.

When your ways please Me, I will make even your enemies to be at peace with you. If you listen to and truly obey My voice and do everything I say, then I will be an enemy to your enemies and an adversary to your adversaries. I will send My terror ahead of you, and I will throw into confusion all the people who come against you. I will send hornets ahead of you to drive out your enemies from before you. I send angels ahead to destroy brave warriors, commanders, officers, and anyone who stands against My plans.

I will put to shame and humiliate your enemies. You will search for those who quarrel with you, but will not find them. Those who war against you will be as nothing, as nothing at all. For I, the Lord of War, keep hold of your right hand. Do not fear. I will help you. I have made you into a new, sharp threshing weapon with teeth.

Now, prepare for war! Stir up the mighty warriors! Beat your plowshares into swords and your pruning hooks into spears! To the weak, I declare that you are strong in Me.

Now, advance forward and enforce My triumph, which My Body and Blood purchased for you. My sacrifice on the cross secured everything you need.

I am Adonai Nissi, the Lord Your Banner, Who covers you in triumph! This is your inheritance from Me. I am your banner. I am your triumph. You win. This is My promise to you sealed by **Our Holy Covenant.**

I REPLY

Thank You, Jesus, for Your sacrifice. I remember and meditate on the price You paid for me. The New Covenant, purchased by Your Body and Blood, serves as my weapon for warring triumphantly. In humility, I confess my sins and ask for Your forgiveness. In Your mercy, cleanse my heart, mind, words, behavior, and anything that contradicts Your character and Holy Spirit. Acquit me of my unconscious, unintended faults. According to the greatness of Your compassion, blot out my transgressions. Wash me thoroughly from my wickedness, guilt, and iniquity.

I receive Your promise of triumph over the enemy in my life through Your Body and Blood!

Triumph is my portion. You are the Lord, a Man of War. That is Your Name.

Yes, Mighty God, confuse my enemies! Divide their tongues, destroy their schemes, complicate their plans against me.

I am a part of the Tribe of Judah. Worship is my warfare! I let my sound resound in the spirit realm. As I release my undignified praise, Heaven invades my battle and fights alongside me. When I praise, sing, and give thanks for Your goodness, You set ambushes against my adversary.

My worship confuses the enemy, and they turn to destroy one another.

You rescued me from my strong enemy and those who hated me, for they were too strong for me. They confronted me on the day of my disaster, but You were my support.

With You I can crush a troop and leap over a wall. You encircle me with strength. You make my feet like hind's feet, and I can stand firmly and tread safely on paths of testing and trouble. You set me securely upon the high places. You train my hands for war so that my arms can bend a bow of bronze.

I pursue my enemies and overtake them. They will be shattered and unable to rise again. Nothing can stand before me and oppose me as long as I live, for You are with me. You will not fail me or abandon me.

You have made my enemies turn their backs to me in defeat, and I silenced and destroyed those who hated me. I will be strong and courageous; I will not be afraid or tremble in dread before my enemies for You go with me.

Contend with those who contend with me, and fight against those who fight against me.

Take hold of Your shield and buckler, and stand up for my help. Draw Your spear and javelin to meet those who pursue me. Let those who seek my life be ashamed and dishonored. Let them be turned back in defeat and humiliated when they plot evil against me. Let them be blown away like chaff before the wind with the angel of the Lord driving them on. Let their way be dark and slippery with the angel of the Lord pursuing and harassing them. Let destruction come upon my enemy by surprise. I call upon You, who is worthy to be praised, and I am saved from my enemies.

As I meditate on and gratefully eat Your Flesh and drink Your Blood, I abide in You and You in me. I remember and honor Your selfless sacrifice by observing communion.

Triumphantly, I claim, receive, and apply the blessing of triumph over the enemies in my life because that is what You paid for. I declare that I have triumphed, do triumph, and will continue to triumph over my enemies! May You receive the reward of Your suffering, my King. With thanks, joy, and faith, I appropriate Your crucified Body and atoning Blood. I love You. Thank You, Jesus, for **Our Holy Covenant.**

Scripture references–Exodus 15, Psalm 144, Psalm 18, Judges 4, Psalm 55, Psalm 35, Proverbs 16, Exodus 23, Isaiah 41, 2 Chronicles 32, Colossians 2, 2 Corinthians 10, Ephesians 6, 2 Chronicles 20, Deuteronomy 31, Joel 3, John 6

Visit www.amandahill.org or scan the QR code below. Partake of the elements and then listen to the worship song that coincides with Day #24.

TASTE AND SEE

Have you ever meditated on the promise that He will contend with those enemies who contend with you? If not, take two minutes to consider this, thanking Him aloud for His faithfulness.

The Lord often gives triumph without us needing to pick up a weapon to fight. Ask the Lord to send His hornets ahead of you to drive out your enemies before you even arrive. Write out this prayer.

DAY 25

FEAR OF THE LORD

EXODUS 14:31, EXODUS 19:16, EXODUS 20:18–21

EL ELYON, God Most High

I OPEN

Thank You, Jesus, for Your sacrifice. I remember and meditate on the price You paid for me. The New Covenant, purchased by Your Body and Blood, serves as my weapon for warring triumphantly. In humility, I confess my sins and ask for Your forgiveness. In Your mercy, cleanse my heart, mind, words, behavior, and anything that contradicts Your character and Holy Spirit. Acquit me of my unconscious, unintended faults. According to the greatness of Your compassion, blot out my transgressions. Wash me thoroughly from my wickedness, guilt, and iniquity.

I receive Your promise of the fear of the Lord in my life through Your Body and Blood!

You are El Elyon, God Most High. There is no other god higher than You! I welcome Your holy fear and trembling. I want the fear of the Lord. I need the fear of the Lord. I want to love what You love and hate what You hate. I want to align with You in every area of my life because You are a good Father who deserves devoted awe and adoring esteem.

You are the all-powerful, all-knowing, ever-present God.

There is none beside You, none above You. No one can compare to You. Awesome are You, Most High God. You are the great King over all the earth.

You reign. Clouds and thick darkness surround You. Righteousness and justice are the foundation of Your throne. Fire goes before You and burns up Your foes on every side. Your lightning lights up the world. The earth sees and trembles. The mountains melt like wax at Your Presence. The heavens declare Your righteousness, and all the people see Your glory.

You are worthy to be feared. When I see Your great power, which You display against my enemies, great reverence fills my heart.

Your people, Israel, heard the thunder and saw the flashes of lightning and thick clouds on the mountain. When they witnessed the smoking mountain and the loud blast of the ram's horn, the whole camp trembled in fear at Your awesome Presence.

I will not misuse Your Name or disregard its reverence or its power. Many may profane Your Name, but I choose to revere it. I will reverently use and call on Your Name, for Your Name is Holy and full of authority.

As I read Your Word, let reverence fill my being, knowing that these are not just stories, but truths about You, Your power, Your character, and Your Kingdom. Let great fear and awe grip my heart so that I will not become familiar with Your Presence or take Your power for granted. Forgive me for areas where I have treated You as common instead of Holy, familiar instead of divine.

Baptize me in a fresh, holy fear of who You are.

May I always remain in awe of Your presence. You call me Your friend because I honor and revere You. In response, You reveal the depths of Your covenant to me, unveiling the profound mysteries and promises found within Your Word.

I will worship You with awe-filled reverence and profound respect. I commit to walking in all Your ways, loving You, and fervently serving You with all my heart, soul, and spirit.

I declare that Your Spirit rests on me: the spirit of wisdom and understanding, the spirit of counsel and strength, the spirit of knowledge, and the reverential and obedient fear of the Lord. I will take delight in the fear of the Lord.

You are infinitely separated and far above all other things. You are not limited. Forgive me for downplaying just how great and awesome You are. There is none more lovely, majestic, noble, kind, amazing, powerful, sovereign, humble, invincible, generous, worthy, royal, wonderful, just, holy, merciful, glorious, selfless, priceless, constant, divine, faultless, or faithful than You.

Your attributes cause holy awe to arise within my spirit.

The fear of the Lord is my treasure.

The more I embrace Your Word, the more I encounter You. The more I encounter You, the more I see the greatness of Your glory. The more I see the greatness of Your glory, the more I love You. The more I love You, the more I fear You.

Let me be keenly aware that You see everything. You are always watching, even when I think I am not being seen. Nothing escapes Your sight. I will live my life with profound admiration for my audience of One.

As I grow in Your Word, I also grow in the fear of the Lord. There is always something new to learn about You. Even after I spend a thousand years with You, I will not have even scratched the surface of who You are.

As I meditate on and gratefully eat Your Flesh and drink Your Blood, I abide in You and You in me. I remember and honor Your selfless sacrifice by observing communion.

Triumphantly, I claim, receive, and apply the blessing of the fear of the Lord in my life because that is what You paid for. May You receive the reward of Your suffering, my King. With thanks, joy, and faith, I appropriate Your wounded Body and worthy Blood. I love You. Thank You, Jesus, for **Our Holy Covenant.**

EL ELYON RESPONDS

It is wise to fear Me, not terror-filled, cowering dread, but a deep recognition and respect for Me, My power, and My holiness, which keeps you from evil and leads to wisdom and blessings. Awe-filled respect is the beginning of wisdom and understanding. This fear enables you to understand My ways and assists you in making sound judgments.

When you regard Me as awesome, you will discover My well of knowledge and spiritual insight.

I desire your undivided attention and unwavering focus. I want to overwhelm you with My goodness, power, and majesty. Let Me show you Who I am, so your unrivaled awe will be restored, never wavering.

Recognizing My holiness and authority produce holy fear. Holy fear leads you to obey Me. When you obey Me, I shower you with provision and wisdom. It is to your advantage to desire the fear of the Lord. It will guide you from harm, evil, and danger.

When you have profound reverence for Me, My mercy and forgiveness abound in your life, you are sheltered from the snares of death, and peace that surpasses your understanding surrounds you.

Now, advance forward and enforce My triumph, which My Body and Blood purchased for you. My sacrifice on the cross secured everything you need.

I am El Elyon, the Most High God, Who blesses you with wisdom, knowledge, understanding, and long life because you embrace the fear of the Lord. This is your inheritance from Me. I will bless you with holy fear. This is My promise to you sealed by **Our Holy Covenant.**

Scripture references—Psalm 147, Psalm 97, Acts 5, Exodus 20, Deuteronomy 10, Proverbs 16, Proverbs 9, Ecclesiastes 12, Isaiah 33, John 6

Visit www.amandahill.org or scan the QR code below. Partake of the elements and then listen to the worship song that coincides with Day #25.

TASTE AND SEE

What is your definition for the fear of the Lord?

Ask Holy Spirit to instill a hunger for His Word within you, so that the fear of the Lord may increase in your life.

DAY 26

DELIVERANCE

EXODUS 12:31-33

ADONAI MEPHALTI, The Lord My Deliverer

I SPEAK

Thank You, Jesus, for Your sacrifice. I remember and meditate on the price You paid for me. The New Covenant, purchased by Your Body and Blood, serves as my weapon for warring triumphantly. In humility, I confess my sins and ask for Your forgiveness. In Your mercy, cleanse my heart, mind, words, behavior, and anything that contradicts Your character and Holy Spirit. Acquit me of my unconscious, unintended faults. According to the greatness of Your compassion, blot out my transgressions. Wash me thoroughly from my wickedness, guilt, and iniquity.

I receive Your promise of deliverance in my life
through Your Body and Blood!

I boldly declare that I am delivered from all forms of slavery, sin, religious bondage, oppressive yokes, and heavy burdens. Deliverance is not just my promised portion; it is my rightful inheritance. I command every Pharaoh and demonic taskmaster assigned to hinder, delay, distract, enslave, and deny me to release me from their grip and free me from their chains now. Let me go! My freedom is nonnegotiable, and I command the blessing of complete deliverance to manifest as I remember the sacrifice of Jesus and the power of His wounded Body and worthy Blood.

I am a loving and loyal servant of Jesus, the Messiah, who has called me and set me apart to reveal His wonderful gospel. I was redeemed at an invaluable price paid by the Passover Lamb of God. Freed from the bondage of sin, I now wholeheartedly embrace my life as a slave of righteousness, aligning myself with Your divine will and perfect purpose for me. I belong to You, Jesus. I am Yours, and You are forever mine.

Everything in my life has transformed because I am joined to You by faith. I decree I have been delivered from the kingdom of darkness, to the Kingdom of Light. I have been delivered from, and I have been delivered to!

Jesus, You rescued me!

I wholeheartedly believe that You are the Savior of the world, and therefore, I am a new creation! Through the power of Holy Spirit, I have been reborn and renewed. Every old thing, including my worldly desires, fleshly thinking, and stony heart, has passed away. All the world has to offer me—the lust and sensual craving of the flesh, and the lust and longing of the eyes and the boastful pride of life—have been buried alongside Christ Jesus. This spiritual awakening has brought new life, and now everything is new!

It is for this glorious freedom that You have set me free, Jesus. You have liberated me! I am thoroughly cleansed, redeemed, and completely set free by Your Blood sacrifice. Therefore, I will keep standing firm and refuse to be burdened again by the chains of slavery and the yoke of bondage.

I no longer dwell in Egypt, nor does
Egypt's mentality dwell in me.

I am called to freedom, and I embrace that freedom, but I will not allow it to become an opportunity for worldliness and selfishness. Instead, I will use this freedom to serve others with love, sincerely seeking their best interests.

I commit to walking habitually in Your Spirit, earnestly seeking You and being responsive to Your guidance. I refuse to carry out the desires of the sinful nature, which responds impulsively without regard for You, Our Father, or Your precepts, King Jesus. I decree that I am guided and led by the Spirit of God. I will not allow the destructive practices and behaviors of sinful nature and its fruit of death in my life, including sexual immorality, impurity, sensuality, lack of self-control, idolatry, sorcery, hostility, strife, jealousy, fits of anger, disputes, dissensions, factions, envy, drunkenness, and riotous behaviors.

Instead, I sow to the Spirit, and in doing so, I will reap the gift of eternal life. I produce the fruit of the Spirit! Love, joy, peace, patience, kindness, goodness, faithfulness, gentleness, and self-control are evident because I am connected to You, Jesus, the true Vine, and our Father, the Vinedresser, who nurtures and fosters my growth.

As I meditate on and gratefully eat Your Flesh and drink Your Blood, I abide in You and You in me. I remember and honor Your selfless sacrifice by observing communion.

Triumphantly, I claim, receive, and apply the blessing of deliverance in my life because that is what You paid for. May You receive the reward of Your suffering, my King. With thanks, joy, and faith, I appropriate Your pierced Body and perfect Blood. I love You. Thank You, Jesus, for **Our Holy Covenant.**

ADONAI MEPHALTI DECREES

My ear is drawn to the righteous who cry out to Me. When you seek Me earnestly, I promise to answer you. I hear you. I hear every whisper and see every tear you shed, and I am faithful to rescue you from all of your troubles. It is My great delight to deliver you from all your fears, troubles, burdens, and distresses. I am your solid rock, your impenetrable fortress, your hiding place.

I am near and attentive to
those Who remember My sacrifice.

What do you need deliverance from? Listen closely! The melodies, echoes, sounds, and songs of deliverance surround you. I, Adonai Mephalti, rejoice over you with exuberant singing, joyful leaping, celebratory skipping, and undignified dancing. Can you hear My songs of deliverance? Can you feel the rhythm of My dancing? Listen closely and feel intently. Let this movement resonate deeply within you, shaking you free from past prisons, the stench of slavery, and brutality of bondage. That is not who you are anymore; you are free.

What the enemy meant for evil, I can turn it around
and use it for your good. I am the Author of the
ultimate plot twist. The enemy thought he had you,
but you are all Mine.

Moses experienced My delivering power. By not fearing, but standing still and keeping quiet, he and all the Israelites were rescued from the hands of Pharaoh and the Egyptians at the Red Sea.

Joshua experienced My delivering power. Through strategy, I delivered the city of Jericho to My people. Listen closely. I am able to deliver you not only *from* something or someone, but also deliver something or someone *to* you, directly into your hands. I am the Ultimate Deliverer.

Shadrach, Meshach, and Abednego experienced My delivering power. Because they refused to bow, they were thrown into the furnace of blazing fire, but I was with them. They were not burned, their hair was not singed, their clothes were not scorched, nor did they even smell of smoke.

Daniel experienced My delivering power. Because of his purity and obedience, I sent an angel to shut the mouths of the lions so that he would not be harmed.

Mary Magdalene experienced My delivering power. I saw her future and cast seven demons out of her. She was the first person I appeared to after I rose from the dead. She was the first to tell the good news about My resurrection.

Peter experienced My delivering power. Due to the fervent and persistent prayers of the church, an angel of the Lord appeared in his prison cell, his chains fell off, and he walked free the night before his scheduled execution.

My desire is for you to not just read about My delivering power, but experience it just like they did!

You may think I am late in your deliverance. Let this be your reminder. I am never late. I am always right on time.

What has been done for you, you are now empowered to do for others. You have been delivered to deliver. Go deliver.

Now, advance forward and enforce My triumph, which My Body and Blood purchased for you. My sacrifice on the cross secured everything you need.

I am Adonai Mephalti, the Lord Your Deliverer, Who rescues you because I adore you! This is your inheritance from Me. I will always deliver you. This is My promise to you sealed by **Our Holy Covenant.**

Scripture references—2 Corinthians 5, 1 John 2, Galatians 5, Galatians 6, John 15, Romans 1, 1 Corinthians, Psalm 34, 2 Samuel 22, Psalm 32, Psalm 107, Zephaniah 3, John 6, Genesis 50, Daniel 3, Daniel 6, Exodus 14, Joshua 6, Acts 12

Visit www.amandahill.org or scan the QR code below. Partake of the elements and then listen to today's worship song that coincides with Day #26.

TASTE AND SEE

What have you been delivered from? What have you been delivered to? Raise a shout of thanks to Adonai Mephalti, the Lord your Deliverer!

Bondage to the enemy is brutal. He tries to convince us through tormenting thoughts that we have not been transformed due to our past sin(s). If this is happening to you, say out loud: "The wounded body and shed blood of Jesus have washed away all of my past, including this specific sin (name it). I no longer live in Egypt or its bondage; therefore, I refuse to allow Egypt to live in me. Satan, your torment has no power over me now. Jesus has forgiven me and chose to forget, and today I also choose to forgive myself and forget my past."

DAY 27

RESTORATION

JOHN 21:15–17

ELOHIM LEHASHIV, The God Who Restores

I BEGIN

Thank You, Jesus, for Your sacrifice. I remember and meditate on the price You paid for me. The New Covenant, purchased by Your Body and Blood, serves as my weapon for warring triumphantly. In humility, I confess my sins and ask for Your forgiveness. In Your mercy, cleanse my heart, mind, words, behavior, and anything that contradicts Your character and Holy Spirit. Acquit me of my unconscious, unintended faults. According to the greatness of Your compassion, blot out my transgressions. Wash me thoroughly from my wickedness, guilt, and iniquity.

I receive Your promise of restoration in my life
through Your Body and Blood!

I will not fear, for You have redeemed and restored me. You are Elohim Lehashiv, the God Who Restores! When I pass through the waters, You will be with me, and the rushing rivers will not overwhelm me. Even when I walk through the fire, I will not be scorched, and the flames will not burn me. I will not even smell like smoke, for You are the Lord. When You act, no one and nothing can revoke or reverse it.

It is impossible for me to be separated from Your love. Tribulations, distress, persecution, famine, nakedness, danger, or the sword cannot come between You and me. In all things, I am more than a conqueror and have triumphed through You because of Your love, which is without rival. You are Master over everything.

I am convinced that Your love conquers death, hardships, demons, fear about today, and worries about tomorrow. Not even the power of Hell can separate me from You. No power in the sky above or on the earth below—indeed, nothing in all creation will ever be able to distance me from You.

> My rightful place is to be seated with and in You, even if I do not always feel it.

You restore everything that belongs to me, with interest. When I pray for those who have wronged me, You restore twice as much as I had before.

You are great, and You perform great miracles! Let streams of refreshing flow over what is dry in my life. Let the tears I have sown become seeds for my upcoming harvest of joy.

You create in me a clean heart, and You renew a right and steadfast spirit within me. Please do not cast me away from Your Presence or take Your

Holy Spirit from me. Restore to me the joy of Your salvation and sustain me with a willing spirit.

Even when I reject, deny, and doubt You, Your love tenaciously pursues and overtakes me. You are the Restorer of my soul! Your redeeming sacrifice reinstates me to a right relationship with You and restores intimate fellowship with You. You remind me of my calling, even after I fail You.

Thank You for Your restorative mercy.

As I meditate on and gratefully eat Your Flesh and drink Your Blood, I abide in You and You in me. I remember and honor Your selfless sacrifice by observing communion.

Triumphantly, I claim, receive, and apply the blessing of restoration in my life because that is what You paid for. May You receive the reward of Your suffering, my King. With thanks, joy, and faith, I appropriate Your bruised Body and precious Blood. I love You. Thank You, Jesus, for **Our Holy Covenant.**

ELOHIM LEHASHIV REPLIES

Before My suffering at Calvary, My friend Peter denied he even knew Me. Yet in My great mercy and love, I restored him as if he had never sinned against Me. After his restoration, once I ascended, he led thousands to believe in Me, performed miracles, was vital in establishing the early Church, and refused to deny Me a second time. His faith was so tenacious that when it was time for his execution, he requested that his cross be inverted, declaring himself unworthy to imitate My death. Do you see? I am able to restore you to a resolute position.

You may have faced many troubles and distresses, but I am able to revive and renew you! My faithfulness and love did not wear out for Peter, and it will not wear out for you either.

Despite challenges, I will increase your honor and provide you with great comfort because you belong to Me. If you endure suffering, I will personally and powerfully restore you and make you stronger than ever before. I will establish you firmly in place and build you up.

I am the Restorer of all things, even time.

I can redeem and restore the time you have lost. I created time. So time submits to Me. I redeem Chronos time (hours, days, and years) and Kairos time (opportune or right time moments). I made the sun stand still and stopped the moon for Joshua. I can do anything. Nothing is too hard for Me. Do you need Me to redeem and restore time for you? All you have to do is ask. Be specific with your request. I love it when you do that!

I am able to replace, renew, revive, return, and restore to you everything that has been lost. I am the God Who speaks and suddenly nothing is missing and nothing is broken. I am your Restorer and your Healer. Restoration and healing go together beautifully, and I love doing this for you.

Now, advance forward and enforce My triumph, which My Body and Blood purchased for you. My sacrifice on the cross secured everything you need.

I am Elohim Lehashiv, the God Who Restores, ensuring you have all you need because you are My favorite! This is your inheritance from Me. I will restore you. This is My promise to you sealed by **Our Holy Covenant.**

Scripture reference—Isaiah 43, 2 Kings 8, Job 42, Psalm 71, 1 Peter 5, Joshua 10, Psalm 126, Psalm 51, Psalm 23

Visit www.amandahill.org or scan the QR code below. Partake of the elements and then listen to the worship song that coincides with Day #27.

TASTE AND SEE

What has the Lord restored to you? Recall and write it down below. Be intentional in thanking Holy Spirit for His restoring power in your life.

Do you feel you have lost time? Have you been deprived of Chronos or Kairos time, or both? If yes, reflect on the circumstance and by faith, ask Holy Spirit to redeem and restore it to you.

DAY 28

UNITY

ACTS 2:42–47, ACTS 4:32

ADONAI ECHAD, The Lord Is One

THE EKKLESIA INITIATES

Thank You, Jesus, for Your sacrifice. We remember and meditate on the price You paid for us, Your Bride. The New Covenant, purchased by Your Body and Blood, serves as our weapons for warring triumphantly. In humility, we confess the sins of Your Church and ask for Your forgiveness. In Your mercy, cleanse our hearts, minds, words, behaviors, and anything that contradicts Your character and Holy Spirit. Acquit us of our unconscious, unintended faults. According to the greatness of Your compassion, blot out our transgressions. Wash us thoroughly from our wickedness, transgressions, and iniquities.

We receive Your promise of unity in Your Body,
Jesus, through Your Body and Blood!

Adonai Echad, forgive our foolish, frivolous bickering. We repent of our critical, Pharisaical attitudes, behaviors, and words, all of which are rooted in pride. We repent for engaging in cycles of offense where we hold each other captive with unforgiveness, resentment, and bitterness. Forgive us for placing politics above people and theology above love.

We bowed to culture, settled for apathy, compromised with sin, and negotiated with lawlessness. You see our self-righteousness as worthless, filthy rags. Forgive us for bringing shame and reproach to Your Name through scandals, fallen leaders, and misrepresenting You before the world. We have failed, but there is a rising remnant.

We will stop imitating the ideals and opinions of the culture, conforming to its superficial values and customs. Instead, we will be transformed and progressively changed by the renewing of our minds. Let this empower us to discern Your will, Adonai Echad. We renew our surrender to You, as living, sacred sacrifices. May Your Bride live in holiness, just as You are holy.

May we live in holy unity with You, Father, Son, and Holy Spirit, and with one another.

We embrace humility, submitting to one another in love and the fear of the Lord. We reject schisms and divisiveness. We forbid the enemy from wreaking havoc through misunderstandings or hurt feelings. We bind and cast out the spirit of offense from leaking poison into the pure river of unity. In Your Name, we break the spirit of strife from causing relational drama, and Leviathan must cease from whispering lies, twisting words, and distorting communication.

Forgive us for not being the salt and light we should be. Make us salty once again; make us a source of light for the world once more.

Help us to live a life worthy of the calling You have called us to and placed upon us. Let our lives demonstrate Your character, moral courage, personal integrity, and maturity—a life that expresses gratitude. Move us with compassion to support one another in selfless, unfailing love, with pure humility, tangible gentleness, and enduring patience.

From this day forward, we decree that Your Body will make every effort to maintain the oneness of the Spirit in the bond of peace. There is one Body, one Spirit, one Lord, one Faith, one Baptism, one God and Father of us all, who is sovereign and working and living in us all.

> There is security, immunity, accountability, liberty, purity, authenticity, diversity, equality, credibility, deity, generosity, identity, opportunity, prosperity and stability in our unity.

Let us stand united, for only a united Church can heal a divided nation. Adonai Echad, help us to embrace our differences and celebrate our beautiful diversity. Remind us to be slow to speak and quick to listen. Give us eyes to see each other the way You see us.

Just as new wine is found in the cluster, our spiritual growth and transformation require the community of believers. Remind us of how much we need each other.

Although Your Body has many members, we all partake from one loaf of bread, demonstrating that we are one.

Thank You for this **holy covenant** and the sacred bond we share with one another and with You. Our many-ness becomes one-ness because we become unified in You. We are not fragmented. We are re-membered to one another.

Re-member us, Adonai Echad.

As we meditate on and gratefully eat Your Flesh and drink Your Blood, we abide in You and You in us. We remember and honor Your selfless sacrifice by observing communion.

Triumphantly, we claim, receive, and apply the blessing of unity in Your Body because that is what You paid for. May You receive the reward of Your suffering, our King. With thanks, joy, and faith, we appropriate Your beaten Body and unifying Blood. We love You. Thank You, Jesus, for **Our Holy Covenant.**

ADONAI ECHAD SPEAKS

Seeing My children living together in sweet unity is truly incredible and fills Me with delight. It is as precious as the consecrated oil poured on the head of the high priest, Aaron, flowing down upon his beard and dripping all the way down to the edge of his priestly robe. This holy unison is like the dew that trickles down from Mount Hermon, streaming down over the hills of Zion. Unity is where I command My blessings. Unity is where I will be found.

I pray for you, My Body, My Bride.

May you be kept in My Name so that you may be one. As the Father and I are One, so you are one in Us. The world hates you because you are not like it. You are in it, not of it. You do not belong to the world. You are not supposed to. I am praying for you, always interceding for you to be guarded and protected from the evil one. You are being sanctified in My truth, set apart for My purposes.

Now, advance forward and enforce My triumph, which My Body and Blood purchased for you. My sacrifice on the cross secured everything you need.

I am Adonai Echad, the Lord is One, Who unifies your hearts and souls with each other, which delights Me! This is your inheritance from Me. I will unify you. This is My promise to you sealed by **Our Holy Covenant.**

Scripture references—Ephesians 4, James 1, 1 Corinthians 10, Psalm 133, Romans 12, 1 Peter 1, John 17, John 6

Visit www.amandahill.org or scan the QR code below. Partake of the elements and then listen to the worship song that coincides with Day #28.

TASTE AND SEE

Do you need to repent for wrong judgments you have made against your brothers and sisters within the Body of Christ? Have you been offended with anyone that you need to forgive and release? Spend some time and discuss this with Holy Spirit with honesty, repentance, and vulnerability.

Take a few moments right now to bring some of your brothers and sisters to the Lord in prayer. Next, ask Him how you can better love, support, and serve His Body.

DAY 29

MENTAL HEALING

EXODUS 15:26, EXODUS 23:25

ADONAI SHOMRI, The Lord My Keeper

I OPEN

Thank You, Jesus, for Your sacrifice. I remember and meditate on the price You paid for me. The New Covenant, purchased by Your Body and Blood, serves as my weapon for warring triumphantly. In humility, I confess my sins and ask for Your forgiveness. In Your mercy, cleanse my heart, mind, words, behavior, and anything that contradicts Your character and Holy Spirit. Acquit me of my unconscious, unintended faults. According to the greatness of Your compassion, blot out my transgressions. Wash me thoroughly from my wickedness, guilt, and iniquity.

I receive Your promise of mental health, healing, and wholeness in my life through Your Body and Blood!

I repent for the sins, known and unknown of the generations who have gone before me. Father, apply the Blood of Your beloved Son, Jesus, to the transgressions and iniquities of my ancestors. I repent on their behalf. Any of their or my sins that opened the door to inflict disease, disorder, sickness, infirmities, and/or imbalances on my mind, wash and forgive them and me, Lord. I command that all generational curses affecting my mental health be reversed by the shed Blood of the Passover Lamb. These curses affecting my mind must now transform into blessings because I have the mind of Christ!

You are Adonai Shomri, the Lord My Keeper. You keep me in perfect and constant peace because my mind is steadfast, consumed, and focused on You. I confidently trust and take refuge in You. My mental health, healing, and wholeness comes directly from concentrating on and trusting in You.

You are Adonai Shomri, the Lord My Keeper. You keep Your Word to me. It cannot return void, but must accomplish its purpose.

You are Adonai Shomri, the Lord My Keeper. You keep me and all that has been placed in Your hands safe and secure until I stand before You on that Great Day.

I confess that I am not double-minded, half-hearted, or wavering in my mental faculties. I am not unstable in my mind or in making decisions. I resist the enemy's demonic forces that would attempt to attack my mind. I wear the helmet of salvation, which protects my mind from his schemes. I am not vulnerable to the enemy's lies, negative thoughts, and fleshly temptations. I identify with You, Jesus, the Passover Lamb, and I am confident in and through You.

I will rejoice in You always. I will not be anxious or worried about anything, but in everything, in every circumstance and situation, I will continue to make my specific requests known to You by prayer and petition with thanksgiving.

Your peace reassures my heart and transcends my understanding, stands guard over my heart and mind. This kind of all surpassing, indescribable peace is what sets me apart from the rest of the world. Your Presence is so powerful in me that anything associated with darkness or the enemy is prohibited in my mind and thought life. I command my mind to submit to Your Spirit.

I have Your mind, Your thoughts, and Your purposes.

> I will continually fix my thoughts on what is authentic and wholesome, lovely and peaceful, honorable and admirable, beautiful and respectful, pure and holy, merciful and kind. I will focus on Your glorious works and praise Your Name always. I will think continually on these things, centering my mind on You and embedding Your truth in my heart.

Rewire my brain and thought patterns, Jesus. There is nothing impossible for You! I open myself to letting go of unforgiveness and bitterness and choose to embrace thoughts of wholeness. I forgive those who have wronged me and those who influenced me to sin. I forgive those who have used and abused me and release them from the impact of their actions and words against me.

By the power of Your Name, I declare that every complicated argument and deceptive fantasy that opposes You is destroyed. Breakthrough is mine as I command every arrogant attitude and every exalted and proud thing that sets itself up against Your perfect knowledge to be annihilated. I take my every thought captive and make it obedient, bowing to Your holy Name.

I speak to my brain and command it to align with Your Word, Adonai. In the Name of Jesus be healed, healthy, and made whole—spinal cord, skull, cerebrum, cerebellum, brainstem, thalamus, hypothalamus, every gland, nerve, cell, matter, and neuron. You are healed and will operate according to the Word of the Lord. I speak to my brain's arteries and ventricles and command perfect blood supply to my brain for proper function. I declare that my brain correctly sends and receives electrical and chemical signals.

Nothing is missing and nothing is broken in my mental health.

Father, I will remember all the works You have performed in my life. Therefore, I command that my skill memory, short-term memory, and long-term memory work in perfect operating condition.

As I meditate on and gratefully eat Your Flesh and drink Your Blood, I abide in You and You in me. I remember and honor Your selfless sacrifice by observing communion.

Triumphantly, I claim, receive, and apply the blessing of mental healing, health, and wholeness in my life because that is what You paid for. May You receive the reward of Your suffering, my King. With thanks, joy, and faith, I appropriate Your bruised Body and atoning Blood. I love You. Thank You, Jesus, for **Our Holy Covenant.**

ADONAI SHOMRI REPLIES

The crown of thorns the soldiers pressed into the Flesh of My skull purchased healing for your mind. You are liberated from all mental torment. My wonderful peace now transcends your human understanding and will guard your heart and mind. I have made you free from every corrupted thought.

I have not given you a spirit of fear, but of power, love, and a sound mind.

You are a carrier of My anointing. Therefore, all bondage, sickness, infirmities, and diseases of your mind are healed. In My Name, all torment from the demonic powers afflicting your mind are broken. I command your immediate release, full healing, and declare that every residual symptom dissipates.

Every mental health condition, psychological disorder, neurological problem, chemical imbalance, hormonal imbalance, brain condition, and related issue bows to My authority including: Anxiety Disorders, Panic Attacks, Mood Disorders, Postpartum Depression, Separation Anxiety, Phobias, Social Anxiety, Depression, Brain Tumors, Bipolar, Manic Depression, Epilepsy, Schizophrenia, Hoarding, Brain Bleeds, Obsessive-Compulsive Disorder, Eating Disorders, ALS, Anorexia, Binge Eating, Bulimia, Stress-Related, Acute Stress Disorder, Post-Traumatic Stress, Dissociative Disorders, Amnesia, Strokes, Dissociative Identity, Neurodevelopmental, Multiple Sclerosis, Attention Deficit Hyperactivity, Autism, Concussions, Aspergers, Learning Disorder, Personality Disorders, Antisocial, Traumatic Brain Injuries, Borderline, Narcissistic, Paranoid, Sleep Disorders, Insomnia, Narcolepsy, Restless Leg Syndrome, Circadian Rhythm, Sleep Terror, Sleep Walking, Sleep Paralysis, Neurocognitive, Alzheimer's, Dementia, and Parkinson's.

Let My fire burn off your stress and anxiety.

Renounce the load of heavy burdens, envy, strife, and every ungodly yoke. Compulsions, confusion, distractions, forgetfulness, mind corruptions, heaviness, weariness, worry, fears, and phobias are not what I designed for you. Receive My perfect love, which drives out all fear. In My love, there is no fear, and dread does not exist.

Mental yokes and oppression slide from you, for I give you My mind and My thoughts. You have a new mind, so trust Me fully to heal it. I heal all the traumatic, tormenting memories of your past, interrupting the continuing loop of pain and confusion in your mind.

Now, advance forward and enforce My triumph, which My Body and Blood purchased for you. My sacrifice on the cross secured everything you need.

I am Adonai Shomri, the Lord Your Keeper, Who loves you deeply! This is your inheritance from Me. I will keep your mind healthy and Whole. I will keep you forever. This is My promise to you sealed by **Our Holy Covenant.**

Scripture references—Isaiah 26, 1 Corinthians 2, Philippians 4, 2 Timothy 1, 1 John 4, James 1, John 6

Visit www.amandahill.org or scan the QR code below. Partake of the elements and then listen to the worship song that coincides with Day #29.

TASTE AND SEE

Are there generational curses of mental illness in your family? Do you specifically struggle with any specific area of mental health? If so, write your answers here and boldly reiterate their complete submission to the Blood of Jesus.

There may have been brain anatomy names that were difficult to pronounce. Holy Spirit hears and understands your declarative intent. Place your hand on this portion of the text and place your other hand on your head. Take two minutes to thank Him for giving you a sound, healthy, disease-free, correctly functioning mind.

Decree for Someone Struggling with Alzheimer's and/or Dementia

Lord, You are ____________'s Healer. I bring them boldly before Your throne, believing that by Your stripes they have already been healed. Your Blood has never lost its healing power. Thank You for Your great kindness and goodness.

Lord, let my intercession rise to You. On their behalf, I repent for their sins, even the transgressions and iniquities in their bloodline from the generations before them. If any of their sins opened the door to inflict this disease(s), please wash and forgive them now, Merciful Lord. By Your Blood, revoke and renounce the enemy's legal rights.

> May all generational curses affecting their mental health be reversed by the shed Blood of the Passover Lamb, transforming those generational curses into generational blessings!

If there has been trauma, mental torment, physical accidents that resulted in brain injuries for ____________, allow your Presence to envelop them now with Your miracle-working power and supernatural peace. By the authority of Your wounded Body and healing Blood, I speak to the spirits of confusion, delusion, fear, and infirmity and command them to go from ____________ and never return. I command the brain cells, ketones, nerves, and neurons that are abnormal to be restored to their original design, the way You created them. Any disruption to ____________'s neurological function and communication, be healed now. I rebuke inflammation, plaque buildup, reduced blood flow, cognitive decline, brain shrinkage, and any other symptom of these demonic diseases. I decree that ____________'s short-term memory, long-term memory, mental clarity, motor functions, ability to learn, walk, and speak are fully healed and restored, nothing missing and nothing broken, never to be robbed from them again. The doctor's report may say one thing, but on their behalf, I choose to read and believe the report of the Lord!

Father, thank You for Your deep concern for __________. I lift their family, friends, and caretakers before You. May they be filled with your patience, compassion, understanding, and great faith as You heal ____________. Thank You that Your Word does not lie and cannot return void. Their healing is finished just like You decreed! Thank You, King Jesus, the Healer!

DAY 30

HOLY SPIRIT BAPTISM, COMMISSIONED FOR SIGNS, WONDERS, AND RESURRECTION POWER

MATTHEW 28:16–20, MARK 16:14–20,
ACTS 2:42–43, ACTS 3:1–10, ACTS 20:1–12

RUACH HAMASHIACH, Holy Spirit

I SPEAK

Thank You, Jesus, for Your sacrifice. I remember and meditate on the price You paid for me. The New Covenant, purchased by Your Body and Blood, serves as my weapon for warring triumphantly. In humility, I confess my sins and ask for Your forgiveness. In Your mercy, cleanse my heart, mind, words, behavior, and anything that contradicts Your character and Holy Spirit. Acquit me of my unconscious, unintended faults. According to the greatness of Your compassion, blot out my transgressions. Wash me thoroughly from my wickedness, guilt, and iniquity.

I receive Your promise of Holy Spirit Baptism and commissioning for signs, wonders, and resurrection power in my life through Your Body and Blood!

Your Spirit, the Spirit of the Sovereign Lord is upon me, in me, through me, and wrapped all around me. By Ruach Hamashiach, I am anointed and commissioned as a messenger to preach good news to the poor, to bring hope to the humble and afflicted. I am empowered and commissioned to bind up and heal the wounds of the brokenhearted, proclaim release from confinement and condemnation to both physical and spiritual captives, and offer freedom to prisoners. I declare that this is Your favorable year, a new season of grace, and a time of great vengeance and recompense on Your enemies.

I am called to comfort all who grieve, to strengthen those crushed by despair, giving them a bouquet instead of ashes, the oil of joy instead of tears, and the mantle of extravagant praise instead of the spirit of heaviness.

I am authorized to work the works that You worked because I believe in You, Jesus.

You said that I will do even greater things because You have ascended to the Father, and Your Spirit lives in me. This is the same Spirit that raised You from the dead, Jesus. All things are possible for me because I believe and trust in You! If there is any doubt or unbelief in me, I ask You to burn it away, up, out, and off me with Your holy fire. Increase my faith, Lord, as I immerse myself in Your Word. I declare that I have confident, abiding faith in You.

I build myself up on the foundation of my holy faith by continually praying in the Holy Spirit. I receive You, Spirit of Truth, as my Helper, Comforter, Advocate, Intercessor, Counselor, and Strengthener. Ruach Hamashiach, You teach me all things, bring all things to my memory, lead me and guide me into all truth and disclose to me what is coming in the future. I embrace Your work in my life, even what I do not understand.

As I meditate on and gratefully eat Your Flesh and drink Your Blood, I abide in You and You in me. I remember and honor Your selfless sacrifice by observing communion.

Triumphantly, I claim, receive, and apply the blessing of Holy Spirit Baptism. I am commissioned for signs, wonders, and resurrection power because that is what You paid for. May You receive the reward of Your suffering, my King. With thanks, joy, and faith, I appropriate Your crucified Body and consecrated Blood. I love You. Thank You, Jesus, for **Our Holy Covenant.**

RUACH HAMASHIACH RESPONDS

Beloved, I charge you this day to go into all the world and preach the gospel to all creation. Go and make disciples of all nations. Teach people to believe in Me and obey My words, baptizing them in the Name of the

Father, the Son, and the Holy Spirit. These signs will accompany you because you have believed. In My Name you will cast out demons, you will speak in new tongues. If you pick up serpents and drink anything deadly, it will not hurt you. You will lay hands on the sick, and they will get well.

I have authorized you to be My ambassador in the earth.

I am the fullness of the Godhead living in human, bodily form. In Me, you have been transformed and complete, achieving spiritual maturity. You know Me intimately and are strong in your faith; therefore, you will accomplish great exploits in My Name.

I have and will continue to pray for you to be sanctified in My truth and set apart for Kingdom purposes. Just as I was commissioned and sent into the world, I now also commission and send you out.

You were made for more.

Can you feel it? You were created to be a mountain mover. Speak to the mountain and tell it to move from here to there, to be lifted up and thrown into the sea. Do not doubt in My power, but believe that what you say is going to take place, and it will be done for you. Let Me clarify this truth. You can speak to Me about your mountain, but I have already given you the authority to deal with it.

It is your birthright to come to Me with extraordinary confidence and boldness and ask Me for anything according to My will. And you know that I will hear you if you ask anything according to My purpose. You know that I hear you and listen to whatever you ask Me, and because of this, you know that I have given you what you asked of Me.

So, ask Me. I want you to ask Me. I am delighted when you ask Me to supply what you need. When you keep on asking, you receive. When you keep on seeking, you find. When you keep on knocking, it will open. I am a perfect Father, and I always give good and advantageous gifts to My children who keep asking Me.

Now, advance forward and enforce My triumph, which My Body and Blood purchased for you. My sacrifice on the cross secured everything you need.

I am Ruach Hamashiach, the Holy Spirit of God, Who baptizes you with My anointing and power, because you are My ambassador! This is your inheritance from Me. I will empower you. This is My promise to you sealed by **Our Holy Covenant.**

Scripture references—Isaiah 61, Mark 16, Matthew 28, Colossians 2, Daniel 11, Mark 9, Mark 11, Luke 17, John 17, 1 John 5, Matthew 7, John 6, John 14, John 16

Visit www.amandahill.org or scan the QR code below. Partake of the elements and then listen to the worship song that coincides with Day #30.

TASTE AND SEE

According to Jude's instruction, take the next five minutes and pray in the Holy Spirit. Time yourself if necessary.

Read Isaiah 61. Meditate on the portions that Holy Spirit highlights to you.

ABOUT THE AUTHOR

Amanda Hill is a prophet, itinerant preacher, author, recording artist, mentor, and entrepreneur whose heart is to awaken and ready the Bride of Christ for the second coming of her Bridegroom, King Jesus. Surrendering her life to the Lord at just twelve years old and stepping into her ministerial calling at twenty, Amanda has faithfully served the Body of Christ across a wide range of ministry roles for three decades. Her fiery breaker anointing, sharp prophetic insight, disarming transparency, and gift for humor create genuine, life-changing encounters with Jesus that engage, uplift, inspire, and equip believers wherever she goes.

Known and loved for a communication style that masterfully weaves the Holy scriptures, Jewish roots, and deep revelation, Amanda preaches with a boldness that shatters strongholds and shifts atmospheres. Having carried the gospel across North America, Europe, Africa, and Asia, she walks out her prophetic mandate in the spheres of business, government, entertainment, and religion. She serves as a trusted prophetic voice to a broad network of churches, ministries, and influential leaders, offering revelatory counsel and Spirit-led direction that anchors and advances the work of the Kingdom.

Amanda and her husband, David, established Kingdom River International in 1998, a non-profit organization devoted to carrying the gospel to the nations. On Father's Day 2023, David graduated to his eternal home, where he backs Amanda from the Throne Room of Heaven as she continues forward in ministry. Married for twenty-five years, they have three children—Mason, Eliana, and Raegan Elizabeth, who dwells in the presence of Jesus. A Charleston native, Amanda resides on a sprawling 95-acre family farm just outside the city.

Amanda is the founder of Amanda Hill Ministries, World Changers Mentorship Group, and Hill House Enterprises, LLC. She is a licensed and ordained minister of the gospel, commissioned as a prophet by Global Spheres Inc., led by Dr. Chuck Pierce, Amanda's Apostle and spiritual father.

OTHER BOOKS BY
AMANDA HILL

Holy Pillow Talk:
Prayers for Intimacy with Jesus Based on the Song of Songs

FOR KIDS:

Not About Me
A Lesson on Humility
(The Adventures of Mandy & Friends)

Free To Be Me
A Lesson on Identity
(The Adventures of Mandy & Friends)

Make It Right
A Lesson on Forgiveness
(The Adventures of Mandy & Friends)

www.ingramcontent.com/pod-product-compliance
Lightning Source LLC
LaVergne TN
LVHW010606100826
845148LV00014B/2871

9781736819043